INTRINSIC GOLF℠
It's Within You℠

How to Play Better Golf When You Don't Have Time to Practice or Take Lessons

By

Bill Denehy

With

Bob Gold

Note: For the sake of convenience, the material in this book has been presented for right-handed golfers. However, we at ***Intrinsic Golf*** believe that the theory and principles found on the following pages will work for all players – especially those weekend golfers who want to improve their game but do not have the time to take lessons or practice between rounds.

Credits: All photographs by Bob Gold and Bill Denehy. The authors would like to thank David Neubacher and the staff of the Windermere Golf Center, Windermere, Florida, for use of their excellent practice facility to shoot the pictures contained in this book.

Note for Librarians: A cataloguing record for this book is available from Library and Archives Canada at www.collectionscanada.ca/amicus/index-e.html
ISBN 1-4120-0008-4

Printed on paper with minimum 30% recycled fibre. Trafford's print shop runs on "green energy" from solar, wind and other environmentally-friendly power sources.

Offices in Canada, USA, Ireland and UK
This book was published *on-demand* in cooperation with Trafford Publishing. On-demand publishing is a unique process and service of making a book available for retail sale to the public taking advantage of on-demand manufacturing and Internet marketing. On-demand publishing includes promotions, retail sales, manufacturing, order fulfilment, accounting and collecting royalties on behalf of the author.

Book sales for North America and international:
Trafford Publishing, 6E–2333 Government St.,
Victoria, BC V8T 4P4 CANADA
phone 250 383 6864 (toll-free 1 888 232 4444)
fax 250 383 6804; email to orders@trafford.com
Book sales in Europe:
Trafford Publishing (UK) Ltd., Enterprise House, Wistaston Road Business Centre,
Wistaston Road, Crewe, Cheshire CW2 7RP UNITED KINGDOM
phone 01270 251 396 (local rate 0845 230 9601)
facsimile 01270 254 983; orders.uk@trafford.com
Order online at:
trafford.com/03-0370

10 9 8 7 6 5 4

This book is dedicated to
my dad Stretch, who introduced me to the game of golf,
to my uncle Ted, who wanted to but did not live long enough,
and to my girls Kristin, Heather, and Marilyn,
who loved and supported me along the way.

In praise of *Intrinsic Golf* – the groundbreaking approach to swing improvement

Intrinsic Golf has made remarkable improvements in my game. Before I read the book and began applying it, I had trouble breaking 90. However, since I started the prescribed regimen, my game has improved. My last two rounds have been 82 and 84. I now have confidence that by simply "swinging" the club, rather than "hitting" at the ball, my shots will be better. And I don't have to spend hours on the practice tee to maintain my swing. I highly recommend it.

Robert A. Fraser
Landscape Architect

Intrinsic Golf allows me to focus on course management rather than on confusing swing mechanics. In less than a month after beginning to use the methods described in the book, I've dropped 2 shots per side off my handicap. It's put fun back into my golf game. I think this concept would even work in tennis.

Jim Maroon
Member, U.S. Professional Tennis Association
Professional Tennis Registry

It's about time someone wrote a book like this. From now on, I'll leave the mechanical swing and the thought process to the pros. I am now pleased with my swing and the results it produces. ***Intrinsic Golf*** really works.

Allan Weber
Attorney At Law

The ***Intrinsic Golf*** method can work for golfers of every level. I was amazed at the swing I already had inside me that this program brought out. What resulted is a great swing that I can repeat, time after time, without a lot of lessons and drills. Improving my own swing and not trying to mimic someone else's – what a great concept.

Brian Blanchard
Supervisor, Guest Services & Admissions
CityWalk at Universal Orlando

CONTENTS

SECTION 2 – THE SHOTS

SECTION 3 – PRACTICE AND EVALUATION

SECTION 4 – THE EQUIPMENT

"A CHOREOGRAPHY

IS DANCED BETWEEN

A GOLFER

AND HIS GAME."

– Ebeling[1]

[1] From The Poetry of Golf by Michael D. Ebeling, Unsoma, Inc.

i. FORWARD BY BILL DENEHY

In the early spring of 2001, while in the middle of a slow Saturday morning round of golf, one of my best friends took a whack at his second shot from the middle of the fairway and hit behind the ball – topping it about 100 yards forward. Before this grounder could come to rest, my friend swung around, made direct eye contact with me and in a very loud voice said, "Can't you come up with some way to play this game without any swing thoughts or mechanics?"

My friend was obviously frustrated and disappointed in his golf game, and he certainly got my attention. At the time I, was a Certified Instructor with a Top 25 golf school company that in my opinion taught a very good system with which to play golf. Having been with the company for more than four years, I saw firsthand the positive results this system could achieve. However, it was mechanical in nature and like my friend, I considered myself to be a feel player.

I wasn't totally dissatisfied with the results I was getting, but I was not very comfortable with how the grip, setup and swing motion felt. I had learned someone else's swing method and I began to ponder whether I could develop my own swing with equal results. Never one to back down from a challenge, I wrestled with what I should do.

Each time I swung a club, I became more uncomfortable with the feel of my game so I decided to separate the business of golf instruction from my personal feel when playing the game. When playing, I needed to remove all the swing thoughts and mechanics I utilized and taught when instructing. Another friend of mine, who has her Ph.D. in Psychology, assisted me by offering me some meditations to help separate the two.

The next step was the hardest. Where would I find my personal swing? How could I learn to understand and feel it? And finally, how could I possibly learn to play without thinking about it once I got to the golf course? Then my golfing buddy added one more question to the mix that made the puzzle even more difficult to solve. How could you achieve all of the above without spending a lot of time taking lessons or hitting balls at the range? Because of his job, which included more than three hours of travel daily, he just didn't have the time to take lessons, go hit practice balls or work on drills at the end of the day. He was the real deal – a weekend-only golfer!

Having been a "Mission Impossible" fan as a youngster, I did what any good problem solver would do – I started collecting data. I collected data on golf schools, teaching facilities, clinics, computer teaching aids, digital video mentoring systems, video graphic simulators, anything and everything on how you could find and feel your own golf swing. What I discovered was this. The library and bookstore shelves were loaded with every conceivable "How To" book and video, and most of the instruction was based on what the "Pros" do. There was also an equal amount of information on the correct golf mechanics. But, unfortunately, there was very little on how to play golf by feel. Nothing I could find talked about how to find and develop your own golf swing. By this time paralysis by analysis had set in, so I thought it would be impossible to play golf, swing-thought and mechanics-free. But I wasn't ready to give up just yet.

I thought about and focused on how a golf school or initial lesson typically begins. At most golf schools, the instructor starts by explaining the grip, stance, ball position, back-swing, down-swing and follow-through of that school's recommended method. At the beginning of the typical first lesson, you are asked to hit some golf balls with a 9-, 7-, or 5-iron and then the instructor makes the changes he or she believes you need in your grip, stance, ball position, etc. As a result, from day one you are trying to imitate and integrate the school's or the instructor's swing mechanics and fundamentals into your swing. In addition, you are constantly being told why you hit shots badly instead of trying to completely understand what it is you do when you hit the ball well. This type of instruction breeds negativity, not positive awareness.

My quest all came together one day while I was swinging a very heavy-weighted baseball bat. I was just swinging it to get loose, to stretch my muscles – to groove my baseball swing. I immediately ran into the house and grabbed my weighted swing trainer and continued to swing. The more I swung the trainer, the easier it became to identify my golf swing. I could feel how my body parts were moving within the swing and I could sense a good swing from a not so good one. Most importantly, I was able to repeat "my swing" hours later on the golf course without a lot of work on the practice range. I had found and was further developing my very own golf swing – one I did not need to analyze, diagnose or change even if the preceding shot was of poor quality. All I had to do was concentrate on the target, feel my swing and swing the club to achieve the desired result. **Without thinking about it!**

All my life in coaching has been dedicated to helping people become better at what they do. ***Intrinsic Golf*** can make you a better golfer because it is the only method that helps you identify your own golf swing and play by feel. The mechanics are your very own. However, it is more than just swinging a weighted swing trainer. First you must be open-minded. You must be willing to swing and not hit at the golf ball, and you must commit to making a minimum of 30 swings a day using the ***Intrinsic Golf*** Basic Swing Development Program (see Chapter 10).

Then you will realize that your swing, like mine, is within you. Trust me – it's there. All you have to do is learn how to find it, understand how to feel it, and then go out and play without thinking about it. Learn to play by feel. Feel your swing and play golf without any swing thoughts at all (zero-nada). Just think of it this way. Do you want to continue playing mechanically or would you like to find a swing that is as effortless and as easy to reproduce as a laugh. Consider this: has anyone ever taught you how to laugh? Do you practice laughing? Doesn't each of us have his or her very own laugh? Of course we do and we also have and can feel our very own swing. Let me help you find it by giving you some input on how you can identify what your swing might feel like. I can't tell you what your swing should feel like, and trust me – no one else can either. But I can help you find it for yourself, feel it and play without thinking about it. That's how you know it's "your swing" – just like you instinctively know your own laugh. ***Intrinsic Golf – It's Within You!***

Bill Denehy
Orlando, Florida

ii. FORWARD BY BOB GOLD

Since the game of golf was founded more than 500 years ago, players have searched high and low for ways to conquer the seemingly innumerable variables that must be mastered in order to achieve even moderate success. According to Chuck Hogan, one of the game's most successful mental coaches, "The trouble lies in the fact that most players try to learn and remember too many things when they play. Faced with all these mechanics, the mind boggles, the brain rebels, and the shot whistles off into the rough."

This quote accurately describes where my golf game was when I first met Bill Denehy. I was barely able to play a round of golf in less than 100 strokes. When I did card a high 90's score, it was due to the fact that I still had a fairly solid short game. However, when it came to full swing shots, my golf game was in shambles.

Like a lot of kids who grew up in the 50's, playing golf wasn't something I did after school. Stickball, then hot rods, were more my speed. In fact, it wasn't until after I served in the Navy and was working full time that I decided to try the game at the insistence of a couple of co-workers. I never took a lesson and I don't recall receiving much instruction from my buddies. I just bought a set of starter clubs and showed up on the first tee.

Although I did learn some basic swing techniques by watching my friends play, for the most part I developed my own swing and within a few years I was scoring in the low- to mid-80's on a regular basis. Then came a 10-year period during which I rarely played due to a vertebra injury from an auto accident. When I did begin to play again, I was awful. I don't know if it was because I forgot my swing, or if I was just afraid to swing, or both. In any case, my full swing game was gone. I took a few lessons. I read some books. I watched some videos. I even hit balls at the driving range (which I never did before). All to no avail since I continued to hit behind, top, and slice many of my full swing shots. Golf was not fun anymore!

That's when I challenged Bill to come up with a method of playing golf without swing thoughts and mechanics that could be maintained by someone with little or no time to practice. And guess what? He did and it helped me significantly improve my game. As a result, when he asked me if I would lend him a hand in producing this book, I said yes without giving it a second thought.

Intrinsic Golf has helped me to both play better and lower my scores. Now I'm swinging easier and the ball is going farther, with a nice little draw at the end of the flight path. What a joy it is to go from being the shortest off the tee in my group to having the longest drive every once in a while. Thanks to ***Intrinsic Golf***, my scores are once again in the mid 80's and golf is fun again.

Bob Gold
Orlando, Florida

PERILS OF THINKING

A centipede was happy quite,

Until a frog in fun

Said, "Pray, which leg comes after which

When you begin to run?"

This raised her mind to such a pitch

She lay distracted in the ditch,

Considering how to run.

Anonymous[2]

[2] From Golden Hours with the Poets by Antelope Publishing.

iii. INTRODUCTION

This book was written after we came to understand that there is really no single perfect swing for playing the game of golf and that developing one's own intrinsic swing is easier to accomplish and repeat than learning to play with someone else's swing mechanics or methods. At about the same time we also realized that millions of players, because of time constraints or finances, do not have the luxury to practice and/or take lessons even though they want to improve and develop their game to its maximum level.

At **Intrinsic Golf** we discovered that not only do different players swing differently, but also that some "conventional methods and mechanics" fit certain types of golfers better than others. Consequently, we found that trying to teach players to use someone else's "methods and mechanics" frequently hurt their ability to play and enjoy the game, no matter how often they practiced or took lessons.

After considering the above, you might logically ask yourself "then how can someone improve their game without spending a lot of time and money to practice and/or take lessons?" Most Pros will tell you that you can't! Don't believe it. Our experience proves that you can – and **Intrinsic Golf** can show you how! But first let us explain a few (sometimes subtle) differences between Intrinsic Golf and Conventional Methods.

Intrinsic Golf	Vs.	Conventional Methods
1. Swinging the Club		1. Hitting the ball
2. Feel		2. Mechanics
3. Speed		3. Power
4. Slow Building Tempo		4. Force
5. Playing Lessons		5. Range Lessons
6. No Swing Thoughts		6. Swing Thoughts
7. Self-Taught		7. Instruction Driven
8. Positive Coaching		8. Negative Analysis Feedback

Read each section in this book in the order presented and don't move on to a new section until you fully grasp the material to that point.

Remember, enjoying the game of golf to its fullest extent is a life-long process and game improvement takes time. You will need to master the **Intrinsic Golf Swing Development Program** setout on the following pages before you will see any solid results. How long does it take? That's up to you. However, our experience shows that if you follow the program religiously, one day you will be overwhelmed with your sudden gain in both distance and accuracy. It's **Intrinsic Golf** and it will happen because all of us have our own perfect swing inside us. All we have to do is find it, feel it and repeat it.

In Section One of the book we describe the **Intrinsic Golf Swing Development Program**. We tell and show you how you can find and feel your own personal swing. We give you some swing motions and physical feedback sensations that will help you ingrain your swing – a swing that you will be able to repeat every time you play golf, without having to employ confusing swing thoughts. We conclude Section One by giving you some basic swing development exercises that will take you less than two minutes a day to do. We also include a pre-shot checklist to help you initiate your setup and swing, as well as a chapter on how to mentally get ready and play a round of golf. Section One is the backbone of **Intrinsic Golf**.

In Section Two we provide some tips and pointers on different stroke-saving shots to use out on the golf course. These are suggestions that should be customized to your **Intrinsic Golf** swing after completing the (daily) basic swing development exercises. We cover Putting, Shots Around the Green, Sand Play, Trouble Shots and Uneven Lies. We also give you some information to assist you in Drawing and Fading the Ball as well as pointers on Practice Swings, Aim, and Posture. The First Chapter, entitled "Reality Golf," puts things into perspective. The facts and figures we share allow you to set reasonable goals and expectations for your Golf Game.

Section Three is all about Practice and Evaluation. We give you drills you can do at home, some while watching TV, and a couple for your backyard. In case you get really inspired, there is a chapter covering The One Day Practice at the Range. Finally, we include the **Intrinsic Golf** Report Card, which you can full out while you play. This simple device will give you the information you need to know concerning the areas of your game that are the strongest and those that are the weakest.

Section Four is loaded with information about purchasing clubs that your pro shop salesman might not want you to know. Did you know that you can "Buy a Better Game with Properly Fitted Clubs?" Certain types of clubs and shafts can turn your slice into a fade or a fade into a draw and others will allow you to use your **Intrinsic Golf** swing to gain additional length and accuracy.

In the Afterword we sum it all up. We put together the physical and mental parts of your game using your **Intrinsic Golf** swing to help you find, feel and repeat your most successful swing motions that will allow you to unconsciously play your best golf – with or without practicing or taking lessons. The only thing you have to do is *stay committed* and do the basic swing development exercises daily. It's the best and most productive investment in your golf game that you can ever make.

SECTION 1 – THE METHOD

"The hardest thing to accomplish in sports is no single act; it is the replication of that act in an endless vacuum of infinite space."

Sandy Koufax[3]

The swing, from address to follow-through, consists of hundreds of separate physical movements, many of which occur simultaneously, and all of which take place in a matter of seconds. The goal for every golfer is to isolate and groove the most crucial of these personal movements, through feel, and then replicate them unconsciously on the golf course.

[3] From A Lefty's Legacy by Jane Leavy

1. WHAT IS *INTRINSIC GOLF*?

Intrinsic Golf is a two-part theory of playing the game that incorporates the following concepts: (1) finding your own swing and playing by feel is easier to learn and repeat than trying to learn and play with someone else's methods and mechanics and (2) that swinging the golf club is easier and more repeatable than hitting at the golf ball. ***Intrinsic Golf*** has four main principles, which are:

- **First, you must find your own swing – *It's within you.***
  Repeated swinging with a weighted swing trainer will identify and groove your own personal golf swing.

- **Second, you must learn to feel your swing.**
  Continued swinging will allow you to uncover the physical sensations of how your body parts move within your golf swing.

- **Third, you must learn to play without thinking about it. Relax both mentally and physically.**
  Trust and accept your swing without any tension or distracting swing thoughts.

- **Finally, have fun. You are *playing* the *game* of golf!**
  Don't make your score the only criteria on whether you had a good day at the golf course.

We at ***Intrinsic Golf*** believe that both the theory and the principles contained in this book will work for all players, especially for those weekend golfers who want to improve their game but do not have the time to take lessons or practice between rounds. And although we do not represent that ***Intrinsic Golf*** will lower your average score to professional tour levels, we do believe that it will help you reach your true potential as a player. And for those of you who do have ample time to take lessons and/or practice, you will find that with ***Intrinsic Golf*** your swing will develop quicker and stay grooved longer than ever before. It has to – ***It's within you.***

2. WHAT IS A FEEL PLAYER?

Would you like to play golf without any swing thoughts? Better yet, would you like to play golf without any swing thoughts using your own swing? Does this sound too good to be true? Well, it's not – it's as easy a 1-2-3. All you have to do is (1) find your own swing, (2) feel it, and (3) play without thinking about it – no swing thoughts.

"Oh sure," you say, "that's easier said than done." We disagree! We believe we come to the game of golf as feel players and are quickly changed into mechanical players. Why? Because there is too much information about the mechanics of the golf swing being taught by too many people via lessons, schools, books, videos, swing aids and swing methods. Everyone is trying to teach his or her interpretation of the golf swing. So what initially may start out as a golf lesson soon turns into a lesson in mechanics.

A feel player, when playing golf, simply moves through four (4) levels: (1) visualizing the required shot, (2) taking dead aim at the target, (3) trusting his or her personal swing to connect the golf ball with the middle of the clubface, and (4) propelling the golf ball, utilizing the correct ball flight and distance, to the target. Voila!

Before proceeding any further, let us give you our definition of feel players. Feel players would rather be shown, not told, what a correct swing looks like. Feel players grip the club in a manner that is comfortable and set up to the ball in a balanced position that feels right for them. Feel players use trial and error to duplicate what they have seen and felt in order to obtain desired results, and they are much more confident using their own personal motion rather than learning to emulate someone else's. Finally, feel players increase their retention through both visual and kinesthetic feedback. This feedback may be enhanced beyond being taught primarily with words alone by the use of video and other learning aids. This can improve the player's understanding of positions and movements, but too much information can hinder their swing development. However, the feedback must be positive (what they are doing correctly), not negative (what they are doing wrong).

Since feel players believe that their perfect swing is inside them just waiting to be released, they trust that it can be found, they have confidence that it can be felt, and they have faith that it can be repeated. Feel players know this is true because they have experienced the swing before, either with a golf club in their hands or in another sport or similar swinging motion.

In this book we intend to provide each player with the necessary conceptual, visual and kinesthetic tools to enable him or her to learn their personal swing feeling, realizing that the word "feeling" may mean something different to each player. Therefore, our goal is to enable each player to easily recognize ("feel") their swing and use it within the limits of their individual anatomy, athleticism, flexibility and physical capabilities. By recognizing ("feeling") their swing, each player will be able to consistently repeat it without a lot of effort and without having to employ distracting mechanical swing thoughts.

Quoting The American Heritage Dictionary, to feel is to "perceive through the sense of touch" or to "perceive as a physical sensation." Taking this into consideration, we believe the easiest way for you to "feel" your swing is to take some swings with a Weighted NRG BALL Golf Swing Trainer (see Page 114 for more information on the "NRG BALL"). With your grip pressure light and your muscles relaxed, move the NRG BALL back with your hands and arms as far as you comfortably can, allowing your shoulders to turn freely as your left elbow bends and your hips rotate without any torque (or coil). Let your left knee move back and up as you gently rise up onto the inside of your left toe. Then, after a momentary pause, return the left heel to the ground and slide the left knee toward the target as the hips unwind and rotate forward. At the same time or slightly before, allow the arms and hands to fall downward as the shoulders turn back into a forward swing, which mirrors the back-swing. Move the club forward as far as you can with the arms and hands while letting your shoulders turn freely. Your right arm can bend as you allow your hips to rotate through as far as is comfortable. Your right knee moves forward while the weight shift of your body pulls you up onto the toe of your right foot. Then it's simply a matter of following through to finish while maintaining your balance. There is but one way to learn the feel of your swing and how fast you can swing before it turns into a hit and that is through repetitious swinging with an NRG BALL.

Now here comes the problem. Most golfers have a desire to increase their distance, especially from the tee box. However, because they typically have never learned the tempo and timing of their golf swing and because they have little or no knowledge of what it takes to achieve distance, they assume that the only way to gain distance is to increase swing speed by swinging the club harder. Therefore, they soon become "Hitters of the Golf Ball" rather than "Swingers of the Golf Club."

The more you swing, the more concentration on the feel of the swing you will develop. Your muscular movements will become more ingrained, allowing you to become less mechanical and swing-thought driven. You will become a more focused, visual, target-oriented golfer who will "let go" and trust your swing.

There are three basic ingredients that allow players to hit the golf ball farther: (1) strength, (2) club length, which increases the swing arc, and (3) flexibility – strength being the least important of the three. A perfect example is Tom Kite. Now on the Senior PGA Tour at age 53, Tom is hitting the golf ball farther than he ever did on the regular tour when he was much younger. Sure, equipment has helped, but Tom regularly works out and endorses a flexibility fitness product.

Therefore, if you want to be a feel player, you must accept the fact that you can only swing the club as hard as your personal swing will allow – any harder and it is a hit. You must develop a motion in your swing that's fluid and flowing and will enable you to produce clubhead speed with as little effort as possible. Remember, a sudden jerk, explosion, or similar action in your swing will quickly turn it into a hit and most likely change the direction of the clubhead path. You must feel at ease, not tense and tight.

The simplest way to determine whether a person advances the ball using a swing or a hit is to look at their back-swing. If their back-swing is <u>noticeably slower</u> than their down-swing – it's a hit! If the speed and tempo of their back-swing and down-swing are similar – it's a swing! Think of it as dancing with your club within the tempo of your swing. Wouldn't you rather make a slow and graceful move like a ballroom dancer rather than a quick and jerky one like a jitterbug? Hopefully, you now have a sense for what we mean by "feel" – so let's move on.

3. WHAT IS A SWING AND DO I ALREADY HAVE ONE?

The last conceptual part of ***Intrinsic Golf*** is the understanding of swing. Let us refer once again to The American Heritage Dictionary, where we find the following definition of swing: "to move rhythmically back and forth as if suspended." In golf, the swing is nothing more than moving rhythmically from a starting position to a finishing position through a weight-shift, turn-back and cock, followed by a weight-shift, turn-through and re-cock.

A swing has a distinct form. Its motion is almost circular and it produces power through centrifugal force. In the golf motion, the swing can change plane depending on posture and lie from club to club. It can move backward and forward slightly, but the motion and speed should remain similar in both the back-swing and down-swing. A motion that goes back very slowly and then moves down and forward quickly is a hit, not a swing. A perfect example of a good swing is a clock pendulum. You can demonstrate this movement by holding a golf club at its grip end with your thumb and index finger and allowing it to move back and forth freely. The movement should be gradual and smooth, not quick and jerky.

The golf swing is a smooth, natural action made up of a series of physical moves that should only be broken down for feel, not analysis. You can feel parts of the swing, but only as part of the whole swing. The swing can be slow, fast, really slow, or really fast, as long as it stays consistent in shape and tempo. The swing can also move from inside to outside or outside to inside or from a flat to upright plane and it can be modified to produce a variety of shots. We believe that once you identify, feel, and repeat your own personal swing, it will be almost impossible to lose it – just like riding a bike. You will find that the centrifugal force of a balanced, rhythmic swing can easily propel a golf ball farther and more accurately than you can by pounding or hitting it with a violent force.

In order to achieve consistency in your personal golf swing, you must strive to conform to the definition of swing we referred to earlier, "to move rhythmically back and forth as if suspended." In *Intrinsic Golf*, that means you should initiate your swing by hovering the golf club at address on all your tee shots (Figure 3.1). Hovering the golf club will enhance your personal swing rhythm in three ways. First, it will prevent stubbing the grass or abruptly lifting the club during the back-swing. Second, it will help your tempo by allowing you to move the club back smoothly. And third, it will help you feel the clubhead, which in turn will allow you to relieve tension throughout the swing.

Figure 3.1

The great Jack Nicklaus, who hovers the club on every shot, was once asked, "How close to the ball and ground do you position the clubhead?" Jack replied, *"As close to the ball and ground as my nerves will permit today!"*

Yes, you already have your own swing inside you. Just swing the NRG BALL a minimum of 30 times a day (see Chapter 12), hover the golf club on your tee shots, and your swing will appear. When it appears, just learn to feel it and all of its moving parts and then just repeat it in a relaxed state of mind. Dave Pelz, the noted short game guru, states "anytime you stay stationary over a shot for more than five seconds, swing thoughts will creep into your mind." So keep moving. Don't allow yourself to stop and freeze over the shot.

In his book Golf Begins at 50, Gary Player[4] tells us "all of the classic swingers from Bobby Jones to Sam Snead had a little move to start their swing." And Gary goes on to state; "I move my right knee inward and shift a little weight to the left foot. This gives me a preview (feel) of the correct impact position, where my weight should be over the left foot. From there I can shift my weight smoothly to my right foot in the takeaway. It's much easier to make this forward-and-back move than to try to start the back-swing from a dead stop." So wag the club, shift a little of your weight from one foot to the other, then initiate that smooth, natural swing that's within you. Trust yourself – it's there.

[4] From Golf Begins at 50 by Gary Player with Desmond Tolhurst.

4. STAND BALANCED AND "AT EASE"

When building your swing, let's think of actually building a backyard swing for a child. The first pieces we would put in place would be the four steel legs along with the crossbar where we would hang the swing. For this exercise, let's look at our feet and legs as the steel legs of the swing and our torsos with breastbone to chin being the crossbar. This foundation must be built first in both the backyard swing and the golf swing before we hang the chains (our arms) and way before we attach the seat (grip the club). Both the swing and your stance must be balanced.

The easiest way to acquire a balanced swing platform is to walk into one. Start walking three or four strides and then stop. Your feet, when you square them off, will be right under you. Maybe slightly toed out, but nonetheless they will be in a balanced position beneath you (Figure 4.1). Now you might want to widen them slightly for more stability, but that's a personal preference (Figure 4.2).

Figure 4.1

Figure 4.2

Just like a backyard swing, most of the weight bearing should be on the inside. From this position we can move our upper torsos to allow us to make vertical or shallow swings depending on the club and shot we are trying to hit. For example, to hit a high drive, we might widen our stance slightly and move our weight slightly back into our rear leg (Figure 4.3). Since we will be swinging our longest club, our through swing will be flatter and slightly upward to hit the ball off the elevated tee.

Figure 4.3

To hit a lofted wedge over a bunker, our stance would narrow from our base stance and we would shift more weight onto our front leg (Figure 4.4). This would give us a more vertical swing and in combination with the lofted wedge, would produce a high, short shot.

Figure 4.4

From this "balanced stance" we walked into, we can make all sorts of personal adjustments to overcome individual anatomy or physical differences. For example, if you are a barrel-chested individual with a large waist and very little flexibility, you might want to see how it feels to flare your toes out and bend over more at the waist to allow more of a back and through turn while allowing your arms to swing freely in front of your chest. If you are a tall or thin person with plenty of flexibility, you might want to feel how a narrow, squared stance fits with your swing.

Swinging the NRG BALL will give you all the answers. Just keep swinging it over and over and feel its path. Feel what your torso is doing. Feel the movement in your hands, your arms, your legs, and your feet and then continue to experience it right back up your body and out your arms to your fingertips. Your swing is there. All you need to do is identify those feelings, enter them on your Setup and Swing Checklist on Page 56, and you will have a starting point to go back to the next time you start swinging.

A perfect drill to give you the feeling of a balanced swing foundation is to sit on a stool with your feet beneath your knees, your arms crossed in front of your chest and the tips of your fingers touching your shoulders (Figure 4.5). Now start swinging your whole body. Turn your shoulders, hips, knees and feet as far as you can to the right, pause (Figure 4.6), then turn your shoulders, hips, knees and feet as far as you can to the left (Figure 4.7). Feel in slow motion how everything should swing in unison. Once you get the feel of this motion while seated, get up and grab the NRG BALL and try to replicate the swing. Over and over, feel the swing and how your body parts react to the swinging of the weighted trainer. You will also acquire a feel for your club path. You will feel if it is going in-to-out, out-to-in, or straight back and straight through. Sometimes even feeling the wrong way to swing can be as beneficial to learning as only feeling the correct swing.

Figure 4.5

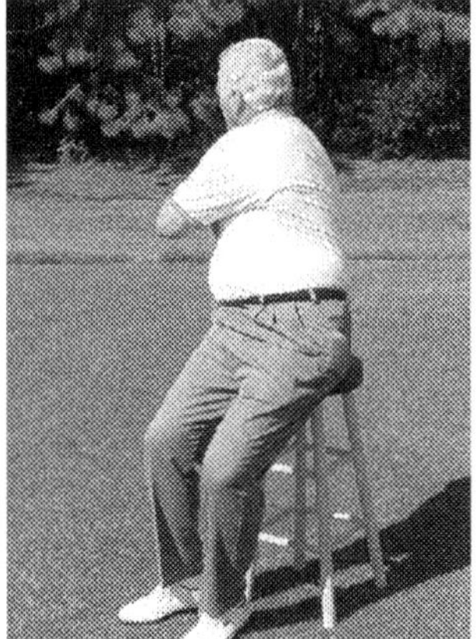

Figure 4.6

Figure 4.7

However, perfect practice makes perfect swings. So concentrate on repeating the path. Watch and visualize this path while you swing. Repeat this swinging day by day until you can feel your personal swing and its natural path. You don't have to force the swing. Just swing and your personal swing and its feel will appear. It has to – ***It's within you.***

5. GET A GRIP! YOURS, NOT SOMEONE ELSE'S

Remember, there are three things necessary to identify your own swing. First, you must find it, and the best way to find it is by swinging the NRG BALL at least 30 times a day for 30 days using the ***Intrinsic Golf*** Basic Swing Development Program. Swinging the NRG BALL will groove your natural swing, whether it's flat, upright, or somewhere in between. Second, you must feel it! The more you swing, the easier it will be for you to feel your arms, hands, shoulders, torso, feet and legs. Feel how they move, turn, slide, glide, lift, pull away and get pulled in. The more you swing, the more you will feel "your" swing. Execute this swing without hitting any balls. Hitting balls will only give you feedback on ball flight that you don't need yet. Finally, clear your mind and let your body repeat this natural swing that you have discovered.

Now that you have an understanding of your swing and what it feels like, let's look at how the grip and your hands can influence your feel and your swing. The grip is the only way your hands come in contact with the club. There is a lot of advice out there on how you should grip the club – in the fingers, in the palm, partially in the fingers and partially in the palm. Some teachers say the palms should face each other. Others say the back of the left wrist should face the target. No, the V should point toward your chin or right shoulder or somewhere in between. Are you confused yet?

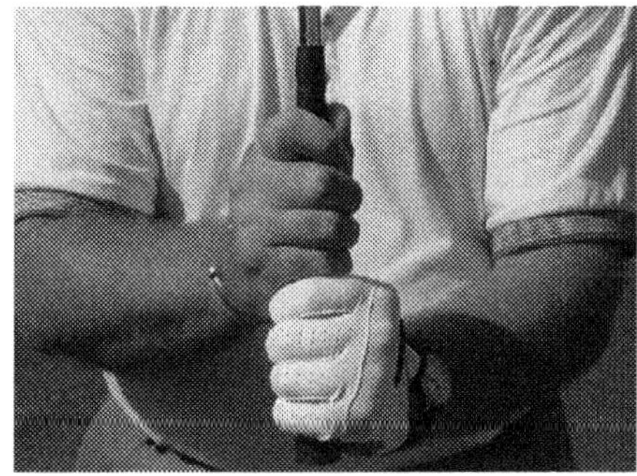

Figure 5.1

The easiest way to learn a grip that you can modify to become your own personal grip is by purchasing a club with a built-in training grip. But first let me describe the four types of grips. The first is the ten-finger grip (Figure 5.1). This grip is sometimes recommended for golfers with small or weak hands and for those golfers who have trouble releasing the club through impact. However, that's not always true. Moe Norman, the Canadian golf legend, who has forearms like Popeye and hands like a vice grip, uses the ten-finger grip.

The second and third grips are called the over-lapping or Vardon grips (Figures 5.2 & 5.3), which only differ by where you place the pinkie finger of your right hand. It is called over-lapping if it is placed on top of the index finger of the left hand and it is considered to be a true Vardon grip if the pinkie finger rests in between the crook of the index finger and middle finger. Most professional players use one of these two grips.

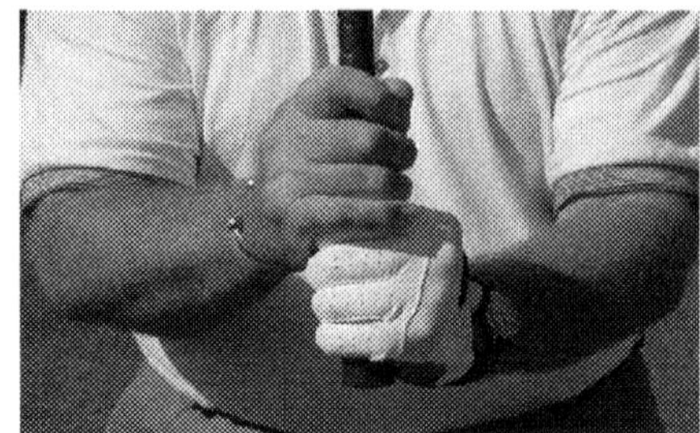

Figure 5.2

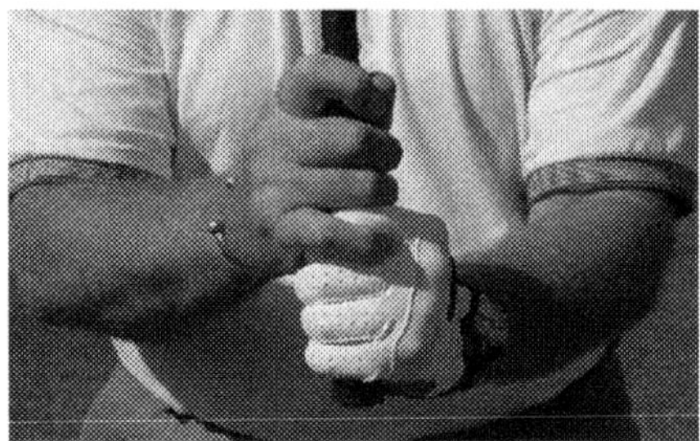

Figure 5.3

The fourth and last grip is the interlocking grip where the little finger of the right hand interweaves with the index finger of the left hand (See Figure 5.4). This is a grip that golfers with small fingers like Jack Nicklaus might want to try. Four other very good golfers also use this grip: Tiger Woods, Colin Montgomery, Tom Kite and Greg Norman. Some say this grip unites the hands better than the other grips.

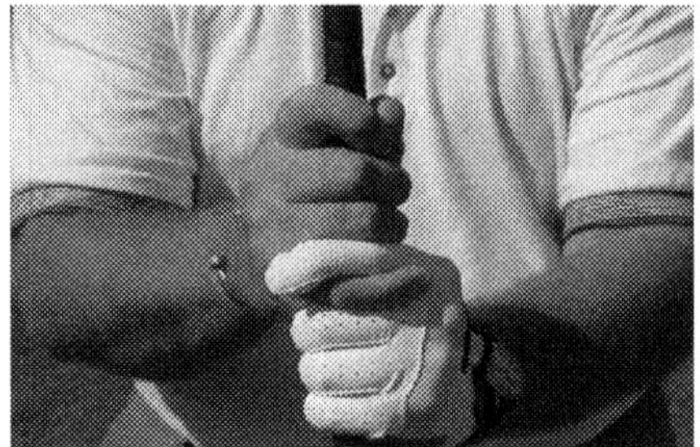

Figure 5.4

How do you know which grip is best for you? Swing a club and get the feel of each one. If they all feel about the same, the answer is “in the dirt.” This means simply that when the ball is introduced to your swing, ball flight and comfort will influence you decision.

After choosing the type of grip you feel is best for your swing, you can then customize it even further. Should you grip the club in the fingers, in the palms, or use a combination of both? Here we go back to feel and experimentation, but now we add one other factor – anatomy. The position of the grip determines the amount of wrist flexion in your swing.

Figure 5.5

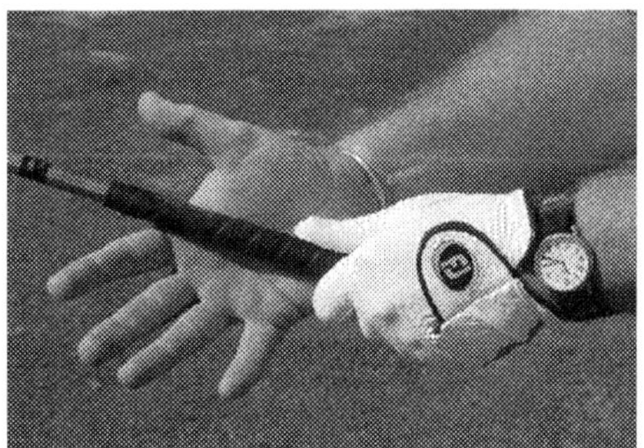

Figure 5.6

A fingers grip (Figure 5.5) gives you the most wrist flexion and promotes the most hand and wrist action throughout the swing. A palms grip (Figure 5.6) creates the least amount of wrist flexion and inhibits excess hand and wrist action.

The combination palm (left-hand) and fingers (right-hand) grip is the grip that is most used by professional players because it gives them the best blend of both (Figure 5.7). Upon introduction of the golf ball to the swing, you will be able to determine whether you need more or less hand or wrist action in your swing by actually seeing your ball flight.

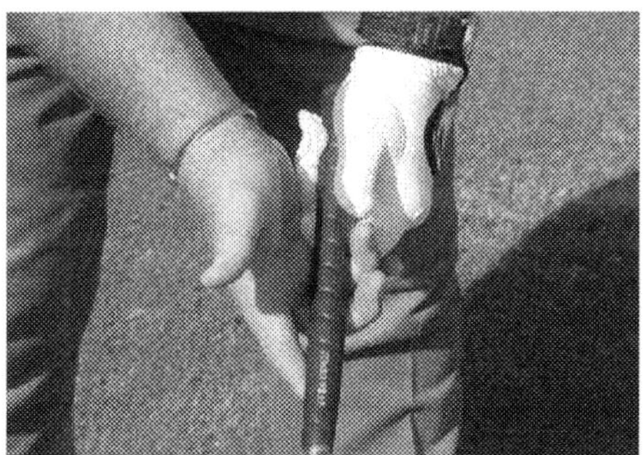

Figure 5.7

To further customize your swing, you need to try and feel which of the three additional grip variations – strong, neutral or weak – best suits your swing. In a strong grip, where the hands are rotated away from the target at address (Figure 5.8), you must position the ball and your hands further back in your stance. The strong grip encourages earlier contact since it squares the clubface earlier in the down-swing. This grip can, depending on path, enhance a right-to-left ball flight.

Figure 5.8

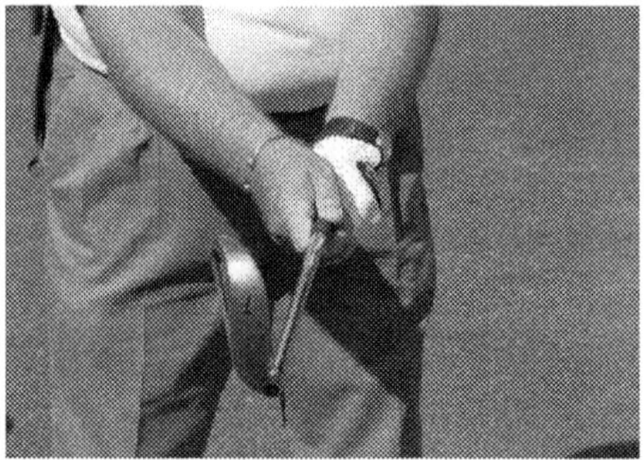

Figure 5.9

The neutral grip, with the V's of your hands pointing toward your chin (Figure 5.9), encourages a relatively straight ball flight and a ball position in the middle of your stance. This gives you the best chance of having a square clubface at impact.

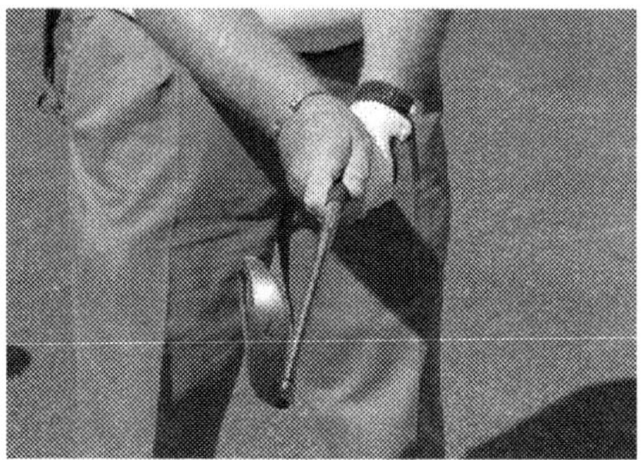

Figure 5.10

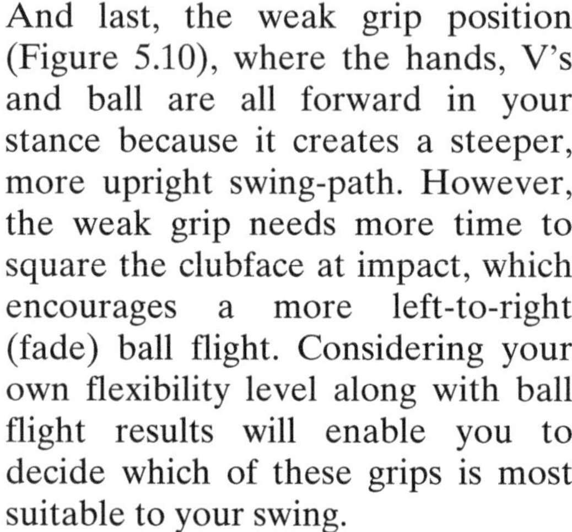

And last, the weak grip position (Figure 5.10), where the hands, V's and ball are all forward in your stance because it creates a steeper, more upright swing-path. However, the weak grip needs more time to square the clubface at impact, which encourages a more left-to-right (fade) ball flight. Considering your own flexibility level along with ball flight results will enable you to decide which of these grips is most suitable to your swing.

Figure 5.11

The last personalized element you need to feel and determine in your swing is whether you place your hands high or low in your stance. Placing the hands high in your setup position (Figure 5.11) allows the hands and arms to roll open during the takeaway, which delays the wrist cock and complements a one-piece takeaway (moving the arms and club away from the ball in unison). High hands also promote a flatter swing plane that is okay for players who have more of a baseball swing due to more rotation in their swing.

Figure 5.12

Low hands at address or setup position (Figure 5.12) promotes an early wrist cock and a more upright swing plane. Golfers with less strength can sometimes develop more power this way because of the bullwhip snap effect it creates. This is most suitable to a player whose swing more resembles a Ferris wheel because of the more vertical swing plane.

There is a right way for you to grip a club. You just have to find it. However, what might be perfect for one individual can be the worst possible scenario for someone else. No one can teach you how you feel! That's why when an instructor starts out by teaching you grip and posture first or has you hit some balls then makes changes in your setup and swing, you are getting a mechanics lesson in a system or method he or she believes in, but you are not getting help in developing your own personal swing. Believe it or not, you have your own swing. You just need to find it once. You can feel your swing and feel what your hands, arms, shoulders, torso, feet and legs are doing during the swing. Then and only then will you be on your way to playing golf with no swing thoughts.

6. SWING WITH YOUR FEET, KNEES AND HIPS

In the swing, you will feel movement in the lower half of your body. Your feet roll from side to side and you rise up on your toes and come back down again. Your ankles roll in and out and your weight shifts from the balls of your feet to the heels and back down and forward. Nothing will kill a swing like dead feet and dead legs. If you don't turn and swing those hips, you will be striking the ball with only a mediocre upper arm hit. In addition to everything else, an upper arm hit looks plain ugly!

While you are moving those feet, legs and hips, you must stay in balance. A good picture to have in your mind would be a speed skater. They move from side to side in a graceful sliding motion, taking long strides but staying in balance. Your feet and legs not only support your swing, given that they are underneath your body, they provide balance and weight shift that produce speed through centrifugal force. Your turn and swing of the hips will also help rotate your shoulders.

Figure 6.1

Here's a drill to feel the swing movement in your lower body. Stand at ease with your two arms and hands in a hand shaking position in front of you (Figure 6.1). Now swing around to the right as far as you can, turning those hips, legs and feet to their fullest extent (Figure 6.2). Now pivot to shake hands with a person behind you. Turn as far as you can to the left in order to shake hands with that person (Figure 6.3). We guarantee that 90% of you have never turned this far back and then this far forward in your golf swing – ever. Some of you will say, "I can't do that and also *hit* a golf ball!!!"

Figure 6.2

Figure 6.3

You are 100% correct. You can only execute this motion and propel a golf ball forward with a *swing*.

Figure 6.4

A hitting motion is almost impossible to replicate time after time, but a swing allows you to move back and through like a hot knife through butter. And now, a crucial piece of information that you must be aware of or it too will break your swing: watch for that dastardly, lazy, cheating front knee. Sometimes we think or mistakenly feel that by cocking our knee inward we automatically turn and swing more in our golf motion. Wrong! You can cock your knee and still keep your front heel down and not rotate your hips (Figure 6.4).

Figure 6.5

And you should not rise up onto the toes of your foot, but instead roll your foot to the inside of the big toe of your foot. On the down-swing, a quick turn back of the knee can pop your front hip open (Figure 6.5) and start a motion that will leave your shoulders dragging the clubhead well behind you. It will also give you a false sense of turning. Rolling your foot down accentuates the correct rotation of the swing. Keeping the heel down may be utilized in a chipping motion, as we will see later in the book when we talk about bringing the whole swing together. But for the full swing motion, let your foot and knee roll away from the target on the back-swing and roll toward the target on the down-swing to get a feeling of what your feet, legs, and hips do in your golf swing.

Grab your NRG BALL and start swinging. Feel the weight shift from one foot to the other. Feel how your legs slide back and forth while increasing and decreasing their weight load. Feel how the hips turn back and remain level to the ground, never tilting up or down during the motion. Roll your feet as you swing and rise up onto your toes.

Come back down and feel your legs slide forward before turning through. Everything is in rhythm, in balance, in your innate tempo. Never be in a hurry. Just move back and forth, to and fro like a child on a swing. The weight of the NRG BALL will ingrain your swing. Just swing it and feel your swing. ***It's within you.***

7. AT THE TOP, BICEP CURL YOUR ARMS

In a circular swing motion, what do the arms do except keep the arc intact? Do they push back? Do they increase the diameter of the swing? Do they lift up? Pull down? Swing out? Swing in? Or do they do all of the above and maybe more? The answer you should be giving is, "who cares!" However, if you are adamant about having answers to questions like these, you are unfortunately trapped inside the world of cerebral golf inquisitiveness that typically leads to death by swing thoughts.

Let's get back to the swing. Keep the swing in a rhythmic motion and resist the urge to swing as hard as you can. Just a nice, easy to and fro, from back to front, swinging the club back as far as you can. When it reaches its farthest back-swing apex, let it slowly move down and then rise to the farthest swing through apex. Then simply reverse the path and so it over and over, up and back, back and through, to and fro. Your motion should be super fluid, inhaling on the back and up swing and exhaling on the down and through swing. Think of the motion as eggs sliding back and forth in a bowl.

Since the golf swing only takes about 3 seconds to complete, it is almost impossible to tell someone what his or her golf swing will feel like in any predetermined position. What others may feel or tell you that you should feel is impossible to communicate correctly because they can't feel what you are feeling. If there are still some doubters or traditionalists out there who believe feel can be taught, we recommend this easy test. Take three golfers – a young man, an older man, and a middle-aged mother and have them explain to you what it feels like to have a baby. The mother can speak from experience, but can she really convey the feeling? The older man, if he has seen children being born, can describe what he felt, heard and saw, but he has no real personal experience he can really relate it with. The young man will typically have no clue! It is the same with the swing. The more you swing, the more your swing will become grooved. You will start to feel your swing through your body's electrical impulses that will travel to and be stored in your mind. Then you and only you will be able to put those unique feelings into words.

For those of you who still feel uncomfortable about letting go of all swing positions, here are seven that you can have: address (Figure 7.1), half-way back (Figure 7.2), to the top (Figure 7.3), half-way down (Figure 7.4), impact (Figure 7.5), half-way through (Figure 7.6), follow-through and finish (Figure 7.7).

Figure 7.1

Figure 7.2

Figure 7.3

Figure 7.4

Figure 7.5

Figure 7.6

Figure 7.7

Now don't go asking whether the toe of the club should be square, opened or closed in any of the back or through positions. The only important position is at impact and the most important motion is path.

Separated, the arms tell us a story about swinging and hitting. At the start of the down-swing, when the weight of the body shifts forward, both arms should swing the club toward impact. Because of the anatomical location of the left arm, however, this motion of the arms gives way to right-side dominance (right-hand golfer). The whole left side soon swings the club into the impact position. Since most right-handed golfers have a dominant right arm, the weaker left arm forces the left shoulder to fly open in an effort to add force. At the same time, the right or dominant arm, due to its anatomical location, is positioned much more favorably to impart force in a forward direction than is the left arm. Thus when we stop swinging, we start a hitting motion. Or worse yet, we don't even start swinging, we just move directly into right arm dominance, which usually causes an over-the-top misdirected motion that produces a slice.

Let's look at this example to better understand, from a physical law standpoint, the difference between generating force with the right versus the left arm. If we tried to move a stalled golf cart, anatomically our muscles are in a much better position to push forward (Figure 7.8) than to pull forward (Figure 7.9).

Figure 7.8

Figure 7.9

Therefore the front arm, which is closest to the target of the swing, is in the most favorable position to lead the club accurately in that direction. At the same time, the back arm is in a much better position to impart strength and force out toward the target. If you have the athleticism and body coordination to get your arms to work together every time, great! Then you're swinging. However, the average, non-mulligan score of a male playing golf in the U.S. is 97 and our lady friends check in at 104. Since these figures haven't changed in almost 50 years, it's doubtful we are really improving our swinging capabilities. What we are doing is becoming a generation of hitters. Whack it, smash it, hit it – we have lost the grace and accuracy of the swing.

Our dilemma is that even though we might all agree that accuracy is our #1 goal, deep down inside almost every golfer wants to be a long ball hitter. Can we achieve both? Yes!!! How? Through swinging. Why? Because swinging can bring an additional variable into its motion that hitting can't. The swinging motion uses centrifugal force to help it impart, into the clubhead, the entire force and momentum of your body's action. The swinger can then utilize the opposite of the law of conservation, which states that arms positioned away from a rotating axis drain energy from that axis and slow down rotation.

CBS Golf commentator Gary McCord compares the golf swing to an ice-skater's spin[5]. When ice skaters go into a spin with their arms outstretched and then pull their arms in close to their body (center of gravity), tremendous rotation results. Similarly, this result can be achieved in the golf swing by pulling our arms in close to our body as we swing through the shot (Figures 7.10 & 7.11). In this manner, a swinger can take advantage of both centrifugal force and reverse conservation of angular momentum while a hitter cannot. The reason is that in order to hit, the motion (leverage or push into the ball) must be going out and away from the center of gravity (our torso in golf).

Figure 7.10

Figure 7.11

The easiest way to utilize both methods of power is by finishing your back-swing with a two-arm bicep curl (Figure 7.12). Then, swinging the clubhead outward toward your target to obtain maximum centrifugal force and then bicep-curling both arms after impact will produce maximum rotational speed (Figure 7.13).

Figure 7.12

All through your swing, notice how it feels to bicep curl your arms on the way back and on the way through. *In addition, on both the back-swing and the down-swing, you will notice that each arm is bent – not straight.* The more you develop your swing, the farther and straighter you will hit the golf ball, because soft arms increase your speed through impact.

Figure 7.13

Now comes the simple mental analogy for you analytical types. The major difference between hitting a golf ball and swinging the club is that *with swinging there is less of a suggestion of power and more of a suggestion of speed.* Both get the job done, but the swing will always be more consistent due to a variety of factors including athleticism, flexibility, age, and sometimes, pain.

[5] From Watson's Shortcuts by Tom Watson with Nick Seitz, Golf Digest, November 2001.

8. DANCE WITH YOUR OWN SWING – RHYTHM & TEMPO

This chapter deals with your inner clock – your own rhythm and tempo. We already have it inside of us. It can be fast, slow, fluid or jerky – but it is there and all we have to do is fine-tune it to match our swing. *For type "A" personalities, this will probably be the toughest element to change and thereby build trust in your golf swing. You will be making the transition from total aggression to moderate conservatism. From power and force to skill and dexterity – from power hitting to rhythmic swinging. (Note: You will find it even harder to transition from hitter to swinger if you play with heavy, stiff-shafted clubs.)*

Once you acquire the mental serenity to move into this relaxed state, you will find that your ability to swing will be similar to doing a solo foxtrot in the suddenly vacant middle of a ballroom dance floor. Some of you are probably saying: " Oh boy, now they're going to introduce meditation and psychobabble into my golf game!" No we're not, we only want you to relax, enjoy the golfing environment around you (and not just your score) and learn to free your mind of all swing thoughts and mechanical positions.

The simplest way for you to understand what we're talking about is to play 18 holes with a lady golfer who is shorter off the tee than you are, be it your wife or just a friend. Play off the ladies' tees. Let your friend hit first, all the time, and try and hit a shot that will end up right next to her shot (just so we don't get confused, we're talking about a lady who can drive the ball a reasonable distance into the fairway and then on her second shot advance it close to the green). On the drive, match her drive distance (you typically won't be able to use your driver since the ball would travel too far) and on your approach shot, you should use a higher lofted club to match her shot distance. What you will soon discover is that your rhythm and tempo will be slower, more graceful, and much more of a swing than a hit. Additionally, your concentration will be more relaxed and focused on the task at hand, which is simply to match her shot distance. Over-clubbing will slow down your swing even more. If the distance dictates a wedge, use an 8- or 9-iron.

To paraphrase Dr. Bob Rotella, a noted golf psychologist, what usually differentiates a person with a mechanical mindset from one who has a feel mindset is a conscious effort to control everything in life. The characteristics are trying too hard, trying to make it happen, trying to take charge and willfully trying to produce intensity, over-concentration and perfect forced effort. This type of thinking is characterized by feedback, judgment, evaluation, analysis and criticism. It is an active mindset, filled with problems, challenges and flaw-fixes. A mechanical mindset is a great motivator on the practice tee, but it can become over-burdensome on the golf course.

The feel mindset involves the willingness to let go of any effort to control any or all parts of life, especially the game of golf. It consists of allowing one's soul to enjoy the activity of feeling each swing and contact with the ball and enjoying the overall experience playing the golf course without any conscious attempt to second-guess, analyze, judge or critique those feelings. It is the complete opposite of a mechanical mindset, which hates making a change because of the fear of making new or additional mistakes or simply looking bad. The feel mindset is a softer, more tranquil, serenity-based mood with positive spontaneity. This inner, quiet state allows you to listen to your feelings and to feel your swing with your body, which will give you the necessary feedback from each of the different body parts as the swing is in motion. While playing, do not concentrate on any one particular part of the motion – just swing the club[6].

To achieve your own personal rhythm and tempo in your swing you must do three things. First, clear your mind of any type of swing thoughts or mechanics and relax. Take 5 or 6 deep breaths and hear yourself breathe. Inhale and exhale and listen to the sound. Second, start swinging back and forth, to and fro, side to side. Feel your fingers gripping the club, your arms swinging loosely from side to side, your biceps curling your arms at the top of the back-swing and at the top of your follow-through. Feel your hips turn and rotate around to the right and then back to the left. Feel your leg, knee and foot being pulled left by your shoulders and hips so that they too swing back as far as they can. Feel the weight shift to the right and your left foot being pulled up onto its toes and back down again. Swing over and over, back and through and then add the third and final ingredient – tempo.

To add tempo, start saying a four-syllable name or phrase to coordinate your swing. Try things like *sup-er flu-id, e-zee does it, John-ny Mill-er, Fred-dy Coup-les,* or *By-ron Nel-son*. The numbers 1, 2, 3, 4 won't work. And neither will 3-syllable names like *Ti-ger Woods, Da-vid*

Toms, or *Lar-ry Mize.* It must be a 4-syllable name or phrase. Just keep swinging your NRG BALL while chanting the 4 syllables. Take note of where your hands are during the chant and replicate the timing again and again. Doing this will ingrain your swing to your own personal rhythm and tempo. Of course, it must be understood that the chant is a practice drill and, as such, it is not recommended for on-course use, unless you do it silently. People will stare.

Remember, the swing is nothing more than connecting a starting position to a finishing position through a weight shift, turn back and cock, followed by a weight shift, turn through and re-cock.

[6] From How To Feel A Real Golf Swing by Bob Toski & Davis Love, Jr.

9. DEVELOP THE FEEL IN YOUR SWING – SHOT BY SHOT

Throughout this book, we have emphasized that the way to develop your swing is to swing an NRG BALL a minimum of 30 times a day for 30 days, *but that's only the physical part of feeling your swing, or one-third of the equation.* The other two parts are the inner state of feeling your swing by concentrating on certain body parts, i.e. feet, hips, hands, and the sending/receiving of mental and physical impulses (feedback) to and from your brain that will interpret what action or motion your body parts are executing during your best swing. And finally, you must move into a state of unconscious consciousness where you completely let go of any and all physical and mental thoughts and/or mechanics, take dead aim at your target and completely trust your swing. With the above in mind, let's start by working on building and feeling your swing, shot by shot.

Putt like a clock pendulum (or with a slight circular motion - arc)

The easiest way to get a feel for putting like a clock pendulum is by starting out with the toes of your feet in a straight line, along with your knees, hips, and shoulders. Bend over at your hips so that your arms hang straight down in front of you, making sure there is a slight gap between your triceps and your chest. This is the only way a putter can be swung straight back and then straight forward like the pendulum of a clock. If you do not normally bend over to hold the putter vertically, then the putting stroke you should use is similar to your other golf swings – circular in shape.

For absolute lower body deadness, keep your knees locked (Figure 9.1). Feel just your arms moving. Back and forth, to and fro, side to side (Figure 9.2).

Figure 9.1

Figure 9.2

Your wrists are straight and firm. There is no cocking or un-cocking of the wrists in the putting motion. To add to your sense and feel of swinging, grip your club further down the shaft and slowly swing it back and forth. Depending on the length of putter you use, your swing will either be straight back and straight through (short putter) or it will open the putter face going back and close it on the follow-through (long or belly putter). During all the time you are practicing your putting swing, make sure you are saying to yourself your 4-syllable name or phrase to help ingrain your tempo (*John-ny Mill-er, Fred-dy Coup-les, By-ron Nel-son*).

You don't want to jab at or hit a putt. Your newly developed tempo will keep you swinging gracefully. Picturesquely hold your follow-through position and pose after you putt – *freeeeze*-frame your swing (Figure 9.3).

Figure 9.3

Here's a tip. Try putting without aligning the writing or any other marking on the ball with the hole and/or target line – that's mechanical. Place the ball down with just the white cover showing and then putt the whole ball toward the hole (Figure 9.4). It takes the mechanics of aiming the ball at the cup out of the putt.

Figure 9.4

B. Chip with your feet and knees

In chipping we make a couple of minor but very important setup changes. We open our stance slightly, grip down on the shaft for better feel, move our weight forward to our left foot and move our hands in front of where we position the ball (Figure 9.5).

Figure 9.5

Feel your weight settling into your left leg. Bounce up and down a couple of times to really grasp this position. Then using your feet and knees, start making little swings back and forth brushing the grass on the down-stroke, making an indentation in the grass. Do this three times to be certain where the club enters the grass. The back edge of the indentation is where you would place the ball in your stance. This position ensures clubface-ball contact.

By having the hands placed ahead of the ball at address, you begin your mini-swing with your right hand in a cocked position and the back of your left wrist in a flat or straight-line position with your forearm. Feel like you dip both of your wrists up to your elbows in cement and keep your wrists in this position all through your chipping swing. For better tempo, hover your clubhead slightly off the ground at address so you don't catch it on the back-swing. Incorporate some body swing. Use your feet and knees to start the motion of your back-swing, and feel your right knee start the down-swing by moving toward the target and pulling and accelerating your swinging arms through the ball. Hold the finish!

Feel like every follow-through is going to be on the cover of golf magazines worldwide. Swing back and forth, to and fro, brushing the grass with your wrists positioned forward in your stance and your weight over your left leg. As you brush the ground, keep chanting your 4-syllable name or phrase to ensure your tempo. If you have trouble with breaking your wrists, then place a shaft down the end of your chipping club shaft so that it protrudes out about 18 inches (Figure 9.6). Begin swinging the club back and forth, brushing the grass below. As you move into the post impact position, the extended shaft will come in contact with your left-side ribcage and will prevent you from breaking your wrists. Use this training aid and you will quickly feel the correct chipping motion. Practice this chipping motion and you will also feel the correct position your wrists and hands should be in all through the chipping swing.

Figure 9.6

Pitch with your hips and add wrist cock

Pitching the ball is probably the toughest motion to acquire feel and to develop a consistent swing for several reasons. First, pitching the ball can involve three different swing-lengths. There are the ½, ¾ and full swings and each of these can produce high, low, running or cutting ball flights. Second, some shots require a dead-hand wrist position and some require wrist cock. Finally, the only way to acquire golf course feel for these shots is by playing them. However, there are two key requisites to good pitching, and they are setting up properly and producing a consistent, soft swing that accelerates the clubhead through the ball. When you are faced with a less-than-full shot, you must think of a less-than-full back-swing. You must be able to feel where your hands move in the swing to produce the shot desired (i.e., hands move to 9:00 on a ½ pitch shot back-swing and finish at 3:00 on the through-swing). Because most people do not develop the short, 50-yards-and-in swing for this type of shot, they take the club back too far and decelerate through impact. Another common mistake is to flip your hands at impact, trying to help the ball into the air.

Figure 9.7

Figure 9.8

The proper setup position is a narrow stance with weight forward onto the left leg. The left foot is flared to the left, opening the hips and shoulders slightly (Figure 9.7). On all shots except the flop shot, the hands are positioned in front of the ball. On the flop shot, the hands are positioned in line with your belly button (Figure 9.8). Sole the club ever so slightly, so as not to catch it in some grass on the way back and start your swing with your forward move and then a hip turn. Your hips turn your shoulders, the shoulders swing your arms and hands, and the club swings back and up.

Figure 9.9

As your hands move back past your right knee, your wrists begin to cock (Figure 9.9). This wrist cocking is the major difference between the chip shot and the pitch shot. By cocking your wrists on the pitch shot, you produce a steeper angle of attack, a more descending blow, which enables you to strike the ball at the bottom of your arc and give it a higher ball flight.

Your hips again initiate the down-swing in the pitch shot. The re-turning of the hips swings the arms and club down with your hands retaining the angle the cocked wrists have obtained during the back-swing, until centrifugal force uncocks them just prior to impact. If you are swinging the club, this action will occur naturally. Don't try to force the action by applying pressure from your right hand to force the clubhead through impact. *That's a hit!* The momentum of your turning hips and swinging arms will pull you around to your left side. A quick bicep curling of your arms will ensure proper acceleration through impact.

The only way to acquire the feel for these different length pitches is to start swinging your NRG BALL the proper distances – ½, ¾ and full swing distance back and then swing forward the proper distances through. A simple mental picture would be as follows. Use the face of a clock as a visual backdrop again. For the ½ swing pitch, your hands should swing back to 9:00 and forward to 3:00 (Figures 9.10 & 9.11).

Figure 9.10

Figure 9.11

For the ¾ swing pitch, your hands should swing back to 10:00 and forward to 2:00 (Figures 9.12 & 9.13).

Figure 9.12

Figure 9.13

Depending on your anatomy and flexibility, you might not be able to swing any further back than 10:00 for a full shot, but that's ok. Just swing your club back the correct distance, pause and actually look to see where your hands are, then swing them forward to the correct through position – at about 12:00 (Figures 9.14 & 9.15).

Figure 9.14

Figure 9.15

Keep swinging until you can verify the correct positions back and through and until you can do them by feel. Swing back and forth, to and fro, using the 4-syllable name or phrase you have picked (i.e., *John-ny Mill-er*) to ensure proper tempo and to ingrain the feel of your swing.

Remember, you must identify your swing, feel it and then repeat it before you take it to the practice range or golf course. There are no shortcuts. Obtaining your personal feel takes time. Time that must be set aside prior to practice of your swing on the range or golf course where negative thoughts, over analysis and ball flight feedback is typically used to judge results.

The whole body swings in your full shot

If you have followed the directions outlined in the sections on putting, chipping and pitching, you should have felt and swung in small increments to reach the full swing. Let's recap ***Intrinsic Golf***'s main tenets. Your personal golf swing is already within you. All you have to do is identify it, feel it and then play without thinking about it. *The swing must be developed before you decide on grip, posture, stance and ball flight.* You identify your swing by swinging an NRG BALL a minimum of 30 times a day for 30 days.

Your swing, due to centrifugal force and repetition, will be identified, felt and stored in your subconsciousness. All your swinging should be at the 4-syllable cadence (*Fred-dy Coup-les*) discussed earlier in this book. Yes, golfers are impatient and want to see immediate results from their efforts, but with ***Intrinsic Golf*** you must slow down and let your swing and your feel develop. As the saying goes, "time takes time!" So don't expect instant gratification. If Rome wasn't built in a day, why should finding and feeling your own personal swing and playing without your old swing thoughts be less time consuming?

During the prescribed 30-day period, you can go to a golf range and/or play golf, but only if you make your minimum of 30 (maximum of 150) swings before you go play. It is of little benefit to swing the NRG BALL 150 times after you have hit balls or played golf. You may be stiff, tired or sore and by doing the swings after your round, you may ingrain a poor rendition of your good swing, or even worse, hurt yourself. We realize that some tour players go to the range and hit hundreds of balls after they play a round. However, we suggest that you relax, go home and start swinging again tomorrow.

All the time you are swinging in your 4-syllable cadence, stretch a little farther back on your back-swing and stretch a little farther forward on your through swing. Don't swing hard or fast. Keep the same tempo or even slow your tempo down a little bit. But keep swinging back and forth, to and fro, making graceful, super-fluid swings. Again, don't stop swinging. Don't take a full swing, then stop and start over again – just keep swinging.

Start your swing with some forward movement, and then from the bottom of your arc going backwards you will feel just your hands moving the club back. Your feet and knees will then start your weight shift back. After your arms pass your right leg and before the arms reach waist high, your wrists will begin to cock. Your hips will continue to turn, which will also swing your arms and shoulders back and upward until they bicep curl and reach their maximum non-forced height. The body weight shift to the right pulls the left foot up on its toe. There is a slight pause, hardly discernable in the universe, before the swing starts back down. Like a majestic building that implodes, the swing moves down from bottom to top. *However, it should be noted that some golfers, especially those who have quick hips that leave their arms trailing behind their body on the down-swing, might feel that their hands should start the swing down.*

The left heel then returns back to the ground, which starts a chain of action that includes the start of a slight weight shift forward led by both knees swinging back to the left as the hips rotate and swing the arms and shoulders around and down. At the same time, centrifugal force pulls the hands and clubhead into impact, accelerating them past the left leg to a position halfway up. *Referring back to the children's swing example in Chapter 6, at the bottom of the backyard swing's arc and at the bottom of the golf swing's arc (at impact), the legs remain grounded. This keeps body rotation – going into impact – at a minimum.* The momentum of weight shift and centrifugal force then recocks your wrists and pulls the shoulders and arms forward until they bicep curl and reach the maximum height of their through swing. Please remember that people feel things differently. You need to identify and understand your personal sense of feel, not what someone else tells you that you should feel. With that said, see if you experience the feeling of your hands moving the clubhead back in the back-swing and your arms swinging the clubhead forward on the down-swing,

The weight shift forward will also pull the right foot forward and onto the toes of the foot. The more you swing, the more you will be able to identify certain parts of the swing, like grip pressure in certain fingers. *But never, ever* should you concentrate on any one part of your swing when you are propelling golf balls on the range or especially on the golf course. The swing is wholeness, a completeness that encompasses the tiniest fabric of the swing into one. If you try to learn and improve each separate aspect of the swing, your attention will always be on analyzing which part of the swing went wrong and how to correct it instead of swinging and keeping a fresh knowledge of what your personal swing feels like. When you just swing and feel your swing with your own personal rhythm, the feeling is effortless. There is no strain, no pain, just a rhythmic movement similar to a tree branch wavering in the wind.

Remember, there are no shortcuts to identifying your swing. You must be able to feel it because it is a part of you, and you must ingrain it so that it becomes repeatable without any conscious effort on your part. Half measures will get you nothing! It's swinging the NRG BALL a minimum of 30 to a maximum of 150 times a day in the putting, chipping, pitching and full swing positions for 30 consecutive days and having faith that your swing will always be there to call upon when you need it.

If you are serious about getting better and improving your golf game, you will commit the 2 to 10 minutes a day it takes to ingrain your swing, one that will provide you with a lifetime of golfing pleasure. Just 2 to 10 minutes a day – that's all it takes.

10. The *Intrinsic Golf* Basic Swing Development Program

This is it – The *Intrinsic Golf* Basic Swing Development Program:

Begin practicing with an NRG BALL by first taking 5 to 30 swings using the Pendulum Putt motion (Figures 10.1, 10.2 & 10.3).

Figure 10.1

Figure 10.2

Figure 10.3

Follow this with 5 to 30 swings using a chipping motion (Figures 10.4, 10.5 & 10.6), a ½ distance pitching motion (Figures 10.7, 10.8 & 10.9) and a ¾ distance pitching motion (Figures 10.10, 10.11 & 10.12).

Figure 10.4

Figure 10.5

Figure 10.6

Figure 10.7

Figure 10.8

Figure 10.9

Figure 10.10

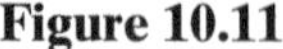

Figure 10.11

Figure 10.12

Then move up to a full swing motion (Figures 10.13, 10.14 & 10.15) and swing the NRG BALL 10 to 30 times.

Figure 10.13

Figure 10.14

Figure 10.15

This will result in your making between 30 and 150 swings each day during the 30-day period. It's really nothing more than you would typically do while warming-up and playing 18 holes of golf, only you can do it in the comfort of your home or office. The entire daily practice routine should take no more than 2 minutes if you swing 30 times and no more than 10 minutes if you swing 150 times. You choose your own routine and schedule based on the amount of time you can spend swinging (minutes) and how quickly you want to improve (repetitions).

11. THE THREE PRACTICE SWINGS

Have you ever seen anyone take a bad practice swing? Oh sure, some practice swings are better than others, but most golfers seem to swing the club better when practicing than they do when trying to advance the ball. Have you ever wondered why?

The answer is quite simple. When taking a practice swing, you swing the club – you don't hit at the ball. You take a relaxed, balanced swing with a swing speed that is typically between 50 to 75 percent of your normal swing speed when striking the ball. During your practice swing, you don't think of mechanics. You have no swing thoughts, just one silky smooth motion back and forth, to and fro, all the time keeping the club above the ground. There is no strain, no pressure, and not an ounce of tension.

In ***Intrinsic Golf***, the practice swing is an essential component in developing and maintaining your personal golf swing. By taking three practice swings before each shot, you will be able to gauge your proper ball position, practice your tempo, and ensure that your swing is balanced. Through these repetitions you will ingrain your swing and ensure consistency of your golf swing path.

Try this to help improve your tempo. Before each swing, lightly tap the head of the club on the ground and then initiate your next swing with a little forward movement as discussed in Chapter 3. Remember, you should never stay motionless over the ball for more than 5 seconds or swing thoughts will creep into your head.

Now it's time to record the rest of your personal setup and swing characteristics so that you will always have a pre-shot starting point that stays consistent as long as you keep swinging the NRG BALL.

12. SETUP AND SWING CHECKLIST

Once you have identified your own swing and demonstrated its repeatability, take a few minutes and record the specific setup and swing elements that form the basis of your swing. Then, in the event you have a problem down the road, you can use this checklist to help you get back on track. (Doing Item #9 constantly validates Items #1 through #8).

1. **Grip (3-Parts)**

A. _____ Fingers	B. _____ Strong	C. _____ Overlapping
A. _____ Palm	B. _____ Weak	C. _____ Interlocking
A. _____ Combination	B. _____ Neutral	C. _____ 10-Finger

2. **Grip Pressure Prior to Swing**
   A. _____ Tight - Last 3 Fingers of Hand Closest to Grip End of Shaft
   B. _____ Loose and Relaxed

3. **Feet (Walking Distance Apart)**

A. _____ Square	B. _____ Open	C. _____ Closed
D. _____ Left Foot Flared-Out	E. _____ Right Foot Flared-Out	F. _____ Both Feet Flared-Out

4. **Hover Club**
   A. _____ On All Shots   B. _____ On Tee Shots

5. **Posture and Swing Plane**
   A. _____ Bent Over & Vertical   B. _____ Upright & Flat

6. **Arms at Setup**
   A. _____ Hang Straight Down   B. _____ Held Out In Front

7. **Head and Shoulders**
   A. _____ Straight Ahead   B. _____ Tilted Away From Target

8. **Arms in Swing**
   A. _____ Straight & Firm   B. _____ Bent & Relaxed

9. **Daily Swing Program**
   A. _____ # of Swings Per Day with Putting, Chipping and Pitching Motion
   B. _____ # of Swings Per Day with Full Motion
   C. _____ Total # of Swings Per Day

13. TRUSTING AND ACCEPTING YOUR SWING ON THE GOLF COURSE

We believe it is extremely important that, before we discuss how to mentally relax and physically slow down our tempo on the golf course, we discuss and accept one major concept: *Golf is a lifetime game of overcoming adversity, and its number one characteristic is that "imperfection is inevitable."* In simple terms it means that every day on the golf course *it's progress – not perfection.* Expect bad putts, chips, pitches, wood and iron shots and treat each of them as just another shot. No bursts of anger, frustration, analysis, or next-shot overcompensation. It's just a bad shot – *FORGET IT!*

Before we actually step out on the golf course, we should warm up properly. That includes warming up your mind just as much as your body. On the way to the course, play some relaxing music. Look forward to enjoying your time on the course. If it's in the morning, see if you can smell the freshly cut grass. If it's later in the day, try to smell the flowers blooming. Listen for the birds chirping, the wind blowing softly in the trees and the warm sun illuminating your face and skin. Don't be in a hurry. Think of each round of golf as the last one you will ever play. You wouldn't want to rush your last round ever, would you? Once you reach the practice tee, do some stretching to further loosen up and begin your warm up. That's why you are there – to properly warm up. Not to whack balls and break a sweat, but to warm up. If you are properly warming up, you should arrive at the practice tee about one hour before your tee time.

Start by swinging your NRG BALL a *maximum of 30 times slowly. Do not swing the trainer more than 30 times at the golf course.* Remember, you're getting loose to play golf, not working on your swing. Get the feel of your swing as you stretch your arc and loosen up your whole body. Feel the path of your swing. And for advanced players, change the direction of your swing from in-to-out and out-to-in and then just straight back and straight through. Swing the club slowly as far back and as far through as you can. Once you have physically loosened up, begin swinging your highest lofted wedge and then swing every other club in your bag, including the driver. Take your time. Focus on rhythm and tempo. Forget distance. *Don't waste your time hitting your driver the most. It's the easiest club to turn your swing into a hit by over-*

swinging. Typically, you only use your Driver 14 times during a round. Practice more with your wedges and short-irons.

When you have completed your practice tee warm up, you should hit some bunker shots and some chips before you finish your warm up with some putting. A dozen or so sand shots and chips are usually sufficient unless you feel you need some extra work in one or both of these areas. When you practice putting, concentrate on three things: (1) tempo, (2) lag putting, and (3) stroking 3-footers – finish off with about a dozen of them. Your tempo is vital on all your putts. It gets the pendulum swing ingrained into your muscle memory, not only for putts but also for the first couple of feet in all your golf swings. The practice of lag putting will help you reduce your 3-putt greens and the session ending 3-footers will help your confidence when you need to hole that length putt to save a par or bogey.

Now you have reached the first tee. You should have only two goals in mind – having fun and driving the ball in the fairway. Swing the club you have the most confidence in – even Tiger hits a 2-iron now and then off the first tee. Take a Mulligan, Hannigan or Flanagan. Play two shots if you want to and playing conditions permit, then accept the results and move on to your next shot. Remember that unless you are in a tournament, you are playing a "game of golf." So make sure you remove your critical practice hat and put on your play hat. If you have time, plan your round. If you don't, at least plan your next shot. What that means is if the first hole is a par 5, concentrate on placing your drive on the fairway in a position that will enhance your next shot. Unless you are playing and practicing golf several times a week, it is downright foolish to think about reaching the green in two and having an eagle putt. So play the hole as a 3-shot hole and try to place your third shot in birdie range. Be happy with a birdie, satisfied with a par and accept a bogey. *Note: We are not promoting taking extra shots (or Mulligans) all over the 18-hole course. However, unless you are turning in your score for handicap purposes or playing in a tournament, having fun and making progress with your swing should be the rules of thumb.*

As indicated earlier, the USGA handicap average is 97 for men and 104 for women, so don't get bent out of shape if your first hole is above par. Take it one shot at a time. Stick with your game plan. Play for position on each shot. Remember, there is only one important shot – this one. What you did on the last shot doesn't make a bit of difference and what you might do on the next shot doesn't matter either. Concentrate all your energies on the present, the shot at hand. Play shots you know you can make, or maybe even some fancy shot you saw on TV or one you pulled off once in an earlier life. However, think each shot through. Pick your target on a drive or even a lay-up shot. Check the lie, terrain and wind. Select your club and form a mental image of your swing and the ball flight you want to create.

Make sure you take three practice swings to gain the feel of your good swing before hitting your next shot. Don't hurry this procedure. Take your time and make three good, slow, full swings. While taking these practice swings, you might want to mentally repeat your 4-syllable name or phrase to give you confidence in your tempo. But other than that, just feel your personal swing glide down the target runway and visualize making ball-clubface contact that propels the ball toward your target.

Stay positive. If you still have trouble clearing your mind, then back off and fill your mind with positive thoughts about your next shot. Talk yourself through and visualize what a good shot should feel like. Start with the grip and internally talk/coach yourself though a good shot. This positive reinforcement will allow you to utilize your intrinsic swing to perform without any concentration on what not to do, which is negative concentration. Then just relax, allow your personal tempo, feel and swing to do their job, unrestricted and accept the outcome as being just part of the process.

Take a couple of deep breaths, hearing yourself breathe and then just trust your feel and swing to obtain the results desired. *Your swing will be there.* You will be able to feel it and your hard work will allow you to forget all swing thoughts and mechanics because you developed a swing you can trust. The only thing left is just to enjoy it. It's ***Intrinsic Golf*** and ***It's within you!*** Good Luck!

SECTION 2 – THE SHOTS

THE MUSCLE MEMORY MYTH

"It's feel you are looking for. Muscles do not move on their own, they need to be stimulated in order to move. They have no brain, no mind, so they cannot have any memory. They simply do what they are told to do through our mental processes. To produce a certain specific movement, they must not only be stimulated for movement, but this stimulation must be directed so the muscles produce the movement desired. Without this direction, the movements produced will vary greatly and will most likely be incorrect for the desired result."[7]

Manuel de la Torre

[7] From Understanding the Golf Swing by Manuel de la Torre.

1. REALITY GOLF

Congratulations, you have completed Section One of **Intrinsic Golf**. If you have been diligent about doing the five exercises that make up the **Intrinsic Golf Basic Swing Development Program**, by now you should have (1) found your own personal swing, (2) felt what your intrinsic swing feels like, and (3) by using the 4-syllable cadence you have also developed your personal swing tempo. You should have also experienced some longer and more accurate drives and approach shots because the **Intrinsic Golf Basic Swing Development Program** has made you stronger and more flexible.

Whether you were a beginner or someone who just became frustrated with your golf game – **Intrinsic Golf** is certain to have made you a better golfer. Are you now PGA/LPGA Tour material? OK Tiger Sorenstam – lets get real! The following facts are meant to get you back securely on earth from your 'this game is easy' euphoria. As Joe Friday of Dragnet would say, "These are the facts, just the facts!"

The average U.S.G.A Handicap for men is 97 and for women it is 104. The lowest average score on the PGA Tour, set by Byron Nelson back in 1948, hasn't been reduced by more than one shot in over 55 years. Of the 26 million people who play golf in the United States, including all Touring Professionals (PGA, Champions, LPGA, Nationwide, Hooters, etc., etc.), only 2 % will shoot par or below, 5% will have a handicap of 1-6, 15% a will have a handicap of 7-20, and 78% (or more than ¾ of all golfers) will have a handicap of 21-30+. So if your only objective in playing the game is to shoot very low scores – you are very likely going to be disappointed! The reality of golf is that without rollovers, preferred lies, mulligans, hannigans, putt raking and gimmies – most players are destined to be members of the 21or higher handicap group. However, if you are now satisfied with your own personal, repeatable golf swing and have experience the social, personal and physical rewards of playing a respectable and consistent game of golf, read on and become even more knowledgeable about the game, its shots and its equipment.

In the 1970's, Dave Pelz, the noted short game guru, began charting the rounds of dozens of PGA Tour professionals. He would walk with them for 18 holes on Thursday and Friday. He would watch both well-known players and nameless rookies, recording every shot they hit. He noted how a swing looked, as well as the result. He watched hundreds of unknowns make the most beautiful swings you have ever seen – then not make the cut.

Conversely, Pelz observed countless well-known players who had ugly, peculiar and unconventional swings, yet they struck the ball constantly nearer to the hole. Pelz soon realized the only thing that counted was repeatability through the impact area. This is the number one point **Intrinsic Golf** makes, "It doesn't matter what a swing looks like – if its your swing, and its grooved, and its repeatable through impact, it is a successful swing!

Charting every shot from hundreds of rounds, Mr. Pelz observed two other interesting facts. First, a PGA pro has only a 50% chance of holing a six-foot putt – and the further away he is, the lower the odds. Think about that. On six-footers, the best players in the world have only a 50-50 chance. Then, for us regular folks, the odds are even worse! Second, a player's chances of getting his or her approach shot on the green and close to the hole, a primary objective if one expects to make birdies and pars, are solely dependant on the player's accuracy with scoring clubs, mostly wedges, from 100-125 yards out. Since 63% of all golf shots are within 100 yards of the pin, it is vital that you improve your shot making in this area if lowering your score is essential to your enjoyment of the game. So what have we learned so far from Mr. Pelz' research?

- Pretty isn't always productive.
- Repeatability through the impact zone is the only true criteria for consistent shot making.
- Accuracy with your wedges is the key to getting your approach shots closer to the pin.
- Even PGA Pro's only make only 50% of their six-foot putts.

In the following chapters we will give you a few simple tips to help you improve your shot making on and around the green. You will learn how to be more accurate with your wedges, how to place your chips within a six-foot radius of the pin, and how to lower your score with either a straight-back/straight-through pendulum putt or a slightly inside back to square and then slightly inside forward putting motion (arc).

2. PUTT LIKE A PENDULUM (or with a slight circular motion - arc)

Whenever I give an individual lesson or teach at a Golf School and we get to the topic of putting, I always ask each student the same question, "how good a putter are you?" Surprisingly, most students answer by saying, "oh, I'm a very good putter – I hardly ever three putt! Unfortunately, if you believe two putts per hole is very good – you are mistaken. Two putts per hole identifies you as an average (or par) putter, not a *very* good one and certainly not a *great* putter. Tour players must average 30 putts or less to be considered a good.

Allow me to do the math. A typical Par 72 course has four par 5's, four par 3's and 10 par 4's. If an accomplished player reaches every green in regulation (par 5's in three shots, par 3's in one, and par 4's in two), and uses two putts on every green, he or she will shoot a score of 72 and will have used 36 putts to achieve the par round. This is due to the fact that Golf Course Architects typically design courses so that putting is exactly 50% of a par score. And if a good player shoots Bogey Golf or 90 and uses 36 putts, his or her putting percentage will still be high at 40%. This calculation begs the following question: "given that putting is 40% to 50% of the game, shouldn't we spend at least 40% to 50% of our practice time putting?" Then why are millions of golfers content to keep blasting away with their driver every time they practice?

Remember the saying "drive for show and putt for dough." Well that old saw accurately describes a major difference between those who remain high-handicappers and those who routinely shoot lower scores. It shouldn't surprise you then when we say, like we did earlier with other types of swings, that you can improve your putting game by using the great putting stroke that's within you – all you have to do is find it, feel it, and then consistently repeat it.

Before we discuss the Pendulum and Arc Putting Strokes, lets take a look at 4 different methods of putting and the advantages and disadvantages of each.

The traditional right-hand low method (right-handed golfers), where the trailing right hand grips the putter below the lead hand, as it is done with all other shots from driver through wedge. The advantages of this method include being both comfortable and widely accepted. However, it can cause more of a hit than the other methods, but is excellent from off the green and on long lag putts. The disadvantages are that due to a strong bottom-hand grip, this method can cause putter face inconsistency and poor distance control, especially if the bottom hand hinges or becomes too overactive. Additionally, this method sometimes causes poor aim if your stance permits an open shoulder line towards your target.

Lead-hand low or cross-handed putting is a method where you use your conventional stance, ball position, and putter length and grip the putter with your lead hand (the one closest to the target) below the trailing hand. This allows the lead arm to pull the putter through impact on a square line while the trailing hand remains passive during the stroke. Advantages – square shoulders at address, which reduces forearm rotation, head-arm-wrist breakdown, and squares the putter face through impact. Disadvantages – takes time to gain touch and feel, especially on long and breaking putts if you're trailing-arm dominates.

The belly putter method is where you secure the butt of the club with your belly or midsection. You can use either the right-hand low or lead-hand low method to grip the putter. Advantages – changes the putting stroke from a "hit" to a "swing". Because you are securing the butt of the putter with your midsection, you always setup the same distance from the ball and it encourages pendulum motion, which eliminates wrist breakdown and minimizes forearm rotation. With this method, players achieve a stable stroke with good control of both speed and distance. Disadvantages - ball Position is critical. Placing the ball too far forward or back can alter the stroke, thus rotating the putter face slightly through impact. Players must also keep their body still or again the putter face will rotate at impact. And, sometimes the eyes are not over the target line, making aim inconsistent.

The long putter method is where the lead arm and hand presses the butt of the putter to the chest or chin and the trailing hand grips the club low on the shaft. Advantages – changes the putting stroke from a "hit" to a "swing" and creates an excellent Pendulum Motion, especially if you hang the putter head above the ground so that it points directly down. Grip and pendulum motion eliminates wrist breakdown and putter face rotation. Excellent directional control on putts if swing is almost vertical. Players can use one arm (trailing) or shoulders to propel stroke. Good for bad backs. Disadvantages –

distance control is sometimes poor on long or lag putts. Putter is unstable in windy conditions and in off green situations. Ball Position is critical because the slightest move of the body can cause putter rotation through impact. And finally, aim can be affected if the player's eyes are farther away from the putt line.

How can you determine which method is best suited for you? There are two ways. First, if you have several putters at home, go to your nearest club-maker and have one extended to belly putter length (41" to 45") and one to long putter length (46" to 50") and try them or go to your favorite golf shop and see if your can borrow/demo a couple of putters for at least a weekend round. The second way would be to go to a golf course putting green and, using putters borrowed from the pro shop, stroke putts with each type of putter in three-foot intervals from 3 to 30 feet and in different directions. In any case, once you have found a successful method of putting that feels both comfortable and repeatable, stick with it for at least six months. It typically takes that long to groove a putting stroke without serious practice.

Notwithstanding the above, we at **Intrinsic Golf** believe there are two more reliable ways to find, feel and groove your putting stroke and that's by using either the Pendulum Putting or Arc Putting methods. However, before we describe these methods, we must make a qualification concerning belly and long putters. There has been ongoing talk that the R&A and the USGA might disallow the use of these methods in the future, so we will stick to the more conventional right-hand low and lead-hand low methods when describing Pendulum Putting.

Now lets setup for Pendulum Putting.

- Decide whether you will use the right-hand low or lead-hand low method.

- Select the putter you will use, considering the type of grip it has. The more active your hands are in the stroke, the bigger the grip you should use since a large grip tends to deactivate the hands and wrists during the stroke and improve accuracy.

- Your feet, knees, hips and shoulders should be in a straight line parallel to your target line.

- Bend at the waist until your eyes are directly over your target line and your hands are hanging directly below your shoulders.

- Bend over far enough so that your hands, arms and shoulders provide a straight-back and straight-through motion, while your hands and arms hang straight down from your shoulders.

- As you bend over, notice that you have shortened the length of your grip on the putter. This helps with control and thereby improves accuracy. You have the option to either use a shorter putter or grip down to guarantee a straight-back and straight-through path.

- Concentrate – take the club straight back and straight through, Square your feet, knees, hips, and shoulders. Make sure there is no rotation in your upper or lower body. Wrists are to remain firm.

- Ball position is one ball forward of center.

- On the follow through, keep the putter face square to the target and hold your finish.

Intrinsic Golf Basic Swing Development exercises 10.1 to 10.3 will help you find, feel and ingrain your Pendulum Putting motion – straight back and straight through. To do this exercise correctly, you must bend over.

Note: For players who are not comfortable with bending over to putt as described above, there is a modified Pendulum Putting method they can use called the Arc Putting method:

- Decide whether you will use the right-hand low or lead-hand low method.

- Your feet, knees, hips and shoulders should be in a straight line parallel to your target line. Flare both your feet out slightly to encourage a slightly in to square stroke.
- Bend at the waist until your eyes are inside your target line with your hands hanging down and slightly forward of your shoulders.

- Ball position is one ball forward of center.

- The putter head does not move straight back and straight through as above, but instead the toe of the putter passes the heel on the back-swing, squares at impact, then again passes the heel on the follow-through.

- Concentrate on a natural shoulder motion that swings the club head slightly to the inside going back and then slightly to the inside on the follow-through. The only time the putter head is square to the target is at impact.

If you move the NRG BALL out away from the shoulders in **Intrinsic Golf Basic Swing Development** exercises 10.1 to 10.3, it will help you find, feel and groove your Arc – inside to square and back to inside – Putting method.

Figure 10.1

Figure 10.2

Figure 10.3

3. FOUR SIMPLE SHOTS AROUND THE GREEN

Paraphrasing the earlier Harvey Pennick quote, "All you need to do to improve your putting is to get your approach shots closer to the hole." With this in mind, here are four shots you can use around the green to place your shots within a six-foot radius of the pin and thereby have the best chance of lowering your score.

The four shots are: (1) The Basic Chip, (2) The Fairway Metal Chip, (3) The Lob Shot, and (4) The 15 – 25 yard, 9:00 to 3:00, Dead-hand Wedge Shot. All of these shots are finesse shots that require a few changes in your setup, grip and ball position. All of these shots call for effortless, crisp, feel swings that are the core of the Intrinsic Golf concept. The goal of these four shots is the same. Achieve maximum accuracy utilizing a to and fro, rhythmic swing – not a short quick jab/hit. Lets take a look at these four shots and some simple tips on how to use them to lower your score.

<u>The Basic Chip</u>

- Change your grip to a weak grip – both thumbs pointing down the center of the shaft.

- Start with your feet together, then pivot both feet towards the target and shift your weight slightly onto your front foot. This will cause a more descending blow. Position the ball in line with your back ankle. Better back than even or slightly forward.

- Move your hands forward so that the butt of the club points towards your front hip. Your left wrist should be flat. Move the club back with some hinge in your wrists on the back-swing (there is no hinge at impact – your left wrist returns to a flat position) and retain the flat wrist in your follow through, which will allow you to trap the ball in a downward arc for crisp contact.

- A great drill is to place a 12" ruler inside your glove at the back of your wrist and secure the ruler to your forearm with a wristband. If you are scooping you chips, you will feel it immediately at the back of your wrist.

The Fairway Metal Chip

This is a perfect shot when the ball lies in light rough around the green. Fairway woods have flatter soles that glide easier through the rough than an iron. They also have less of a chance of getting the hosel snagged in the grass.

- Again, as with all finesse shots, weaken your grip.

- Set you feet in a narrow, square stance to the target. Position the ball back of center, towards the inside of your back ankle. Never position the ball forward of center.

- Grip down on the shaft, past the grip, with your bottom hand at a distance similar to your putter's length. Place slightly more weight onto your front foot to promote a descending blow.

- Now execute a one-piece arms and shoulders putting stroke, keeping both wrists firm during the back-swing, impact, and follow-through. The ball will pop off the face and roll smoothly onto the green.

The Lob Shot

- Again, weaken your grip. Then, with your bottom hand, make it even weaker. In fact, you should place the first knuckle of your index finger on top of the grip after you open the face of the club. Your grip should be very loose.

- Start with you feet together in a narrow stance, which will promote a more descending blow. Position the ball in the middle of your stance and flare-open your front foot.

- Cock your wrists quickly during the back-swing and move to the ¾ swing position. Slide the club under the ball, accelerating through impact and then re-cock the club quickly and finish with a high follow through. Think of letting the clubface pass the hands at impact.

- The extra weak grip with an open clubface and soft hands should produce a high, soft-landing shot.

The 15 to 25 yard, 9:00 to 3:00, Dead-hand Wedge Shot.

This shot, also known as the ½ wedge, is one of the best shots you can use around the green because your follow through (low for running shots and high for a quick stoppers) can be used for a variety of front or back pin placements.

- Again, as with all finesse shots, change your grip to a weak grip – both thumbs pointing down the center of the shaft.
- The ball should be placed in middle of your stance and both feet should be square to target. Move a little closer to the ball and grip down slightly on the shaft.
- Here's the key. Swing the club back so that your hands are at about the 9:00 position, *without hinging your wrists*. Swing the club down, accelerating through impact, with your body – not your hands and arms.
- Think of having both upper arms glued to your chest. Finish the swing at the 3:00 position, *again without hinging your wrists.*

Master these four shots and you are destined to lower you scores, because these too are your money shots. Swing your NRG BALL 5 to 30 times using the Pendulum Putt, Chipping, ½ Distance Pitching, and ¾ Distance Pitching motions shown below (**Intrinsic Golf Basic Swing Development Program** exercises 10.1-10.3, 10.4-10.6, 10.7-10.9 and 10.10 to 10.12) and you will find, feel and ingrain these score-improving shots.

Figure 10.1

Figure 10.2

Figure 10.3

Figure 10.4

Figure 10.5

Figure 10.6

Figure 10.7

Figure 10.8

Figure 10.9

Figure 10.10

Figure 10.11

Figure 10.12

4. SAND PLAY IS JUST "SWINGING AT THE BEACH"

Swinging out of the sand the **Intrinsic Golf** way is as easy as 1-2-3. However, before I give you the three very simple secrets to sand play, let me emphasize what your goal should be – *Get the ball out of the sand with one shot!* If you are in a fairway bunker – get the ball back into the fairway. If you are in a greenside bunker, get the ball onto the green. Too often we have visions of the Tour Player who either hits a 170-yard 7-iron out of a fairway bunker that lands softly on the green close to the pin or holes-out with a lob wedge from a greenside bunker. Remember, the goal is simple – *Get out of the sand!*

Now we are ready for the three secrets to sand play. No. 1, because you are use to hovering your club, this shot is similar to all your other shots. No. 2, because you always take three practice swings (outside the bunker in this case), you know where the bottom of your swing is and can simply address the ball so the club will bottom-out in the sand 1 to 2 inches behind the ball. And No. 3, when you swing, move the club "to and fro", which in bunker play means a complete swing including the follow through. More balls are left in the sand because of an abbreviated swing or "chop" at the ball than for any other reason. So swing the club, don't hit at the sand.

There are some additional considerations to swinging out of both fairway and greenside bunkers that should be mentioned. Out of both bunkers, the swing should be made more with the upper body and less with motion from your legs. Think of the swing as being anchored, which you can accomplish by digging in well with your feet to prevent slipping or sliding during the swing.

Now let's discuss the slight differences between playing from fairway bunkers and playing from greenside bunkers. When playing from a fairway bunker, the lie of the ball and the height of the lip on the bunker are your first considerations. Remember, your goal is to get the ball out! So first select a club that will do just that and then choke up on the club to compensate for the fact that you have lowered your body in the sand by digging in. Now swing "to and fro" smoothly and try to pick the ball cleanly out with as little sand as possible. Swing flat-footed to maintain your balance and follow through. Remember, a slightly thinned shot will always get you out of the bunker. That is provided you have selected a club that allows a safe margin for error – a_club that has a bit more loft than is absolutely necessary to clear the lip of the bunker.

When playing from greenside bunkers, keep your walk-in-stance narrow. This will allow you to deliver a more descending blow that will give you more height coming out. Play the ball forward of the bottom of your swing arc, which you established by taking your three practice swings outside the bunker. Flare your front foot about six inches to the left and point your back toes at the ball. This will help you swing across the ball and cut under the sand to propel the ball upward and forward. Open the clubface and aim the scoring lines at the flag (the scoring lines are the lines perpendicular to and at the ends of the club face grooves). You must do this by re-gripping the club and not through manipulation of the club with your arms and hands. Take a slow, smooth, leisurely swing with just your upper body and slide the clubface 1 to 2 inches behind and under the ball at impact, then follow-through and pose in the finish position. Remember; use a ¾ back-swing and a full follow through. Don't cut the swing short.

When confronted with fried-egg or buried lies, close your stance to almost square and close the clubface. Your swing should remain the same, but the results will be far different because of your set up. Expect the ball to come out low and running. Since your swing will turn into more of a chop, cut down your follow through.

Sand shots are easy if you swing the club and difficult if you hit at the ball or sand. Remember, there are more shots missed by stopping the club in the sand than for any other reason. So swing the club "to and fro" with good tempo, balance and follow through and you will love playing in the sand with your one-shot-out swing.

Here's a review of the **Intrinsic Golf** approach to sand play out of a greenside bunker.

- Narrow you walk-in stance to provide a more descending blow.

- Play the ball forward of the bottom of your swing arc.

- Flare your front foot about 6" to the left.

- Point your back toes towards the ball and dig both feet into the sand.

- Open the clubface by re-gripping the club and aim the scoring lines at the target. Shoulders should now aim left of the target.

- Take a slow, smooth accelerating swing with just your upper body with the clubface entering the sand 1-2 inches behind the ball. Swing! Don't hit at the sand or the ball.

- Full follow through with hands above shoulders.

- Believe that sand shots can be fun in all kinds of sand and even with funky lies.

Two Additional Sand Shots -

- On downhill lies, position the ball back in your stance and use a steep descent into the sand and have your swing follow the slope of the hill.

- On Uphill lies, move the ball forward of your natural lie, make a slow, low takeaway with your weight forward and hit behind the ball.

On these shots, do not worry about a full follow through, just concentrate on accelerating the club the 1 or 2 inches behind the ball and let it pop onto the green.

Intrinsic Golf Basic Swing Development exercises 10.10 to 10.12 will help you find, feel and ingrain your swing for these shots.

Figure 10.10

Figure 10.11

Figure 10.12

5. HOW TO SCORE WITH YOUR WEDGES

I once heard an interesting story about how Tom Kite went to his famous coach Harvey Pennick for a putting lesson. After demonstrating his putting motion to Harvey, they jumped into their respective golf carts and headed away from the clubhouse. They soon came to a fork in the cart path that required a decision – right for the practice putting green and left for the range. Kite steered his cart to the right, but Harvey went left towards the range. Upon noticing Harvey's direction, Kite yelled; "Hey, Harvey, I need a putting lesson!" Harvey replied, "There is nothing wrong with your putting stroke, you just need to get your approach shots closer to the hole."

This chapter is devoted strictly to scoring. Why? The answer is obvious considering these facts as presented by Dave Pelz in his "Short Game Bible:"

- Golf balls fly farther, straighter, and spin better than ever before.
- Drivers are lighter, stronger and longer; irons are more forgiving; and shafts are both lighter and more flexible – all to enable you to propel the ball longer and straighter.
- Greens are smoother, faster and better maintained.
- Yet the average golfer's score hasn't gone down as much as a point in over 50 years.

Our reasons for emphasizing scoring are even simpler. Sixty-three percent of all of golf shots are made within 100 yards of the pin, yet when we do find a little time to practice all we typically do is hit long-irons and woods. We seldom bother trying to improve our accuracy on scoring shots. We seem to be mesmerized by length and power and turned off by accuracy and finesse. Granted, we repeatedly stress speed over power, swinging instead of hitting, and feel over force – but scoring is really the name of the game. "It's not only about how you got there, it's about how few strokes it took you to get the ball into the hole!"

In 1990 Dave Pelz wrote a cover story for Golf Magazine entitled "The 3x4 System." In the story the author recommends the use of 3 swings with each of 4 wedges, which will cover the average golfer's distance from approximately 100 yards to the pin. The 3x4 System was developed after extensive research that proved that both amateurs and pros typically hit their wedges straight, with the difference in accuracy being the knowledge of the distances covered by each wedge with the 3 swing lengths, which are the ¾, the ½, and the ¼ swing. These 3 swing lengths are used with the 4 scoring wedges, which are the Pitching Wedge (45° to 49° loft), the Mid-Wedge, Gap, or Attack Wedge (50° to 53° loft), the Sand Wedge (54° to 57° loft), and the Lob Wedge (58° to 64° loft).

Lets look at the 3x4 System and see how we can incorporate its fundamentals into our **Intrinsic Golf** swing. Follow the steps described below and you will learn how to easily remember the distances you propel the ball with each swing. Additionally, you will learn a simple method utilizing one swing that can cover all these distances. We begin by determining your wedge stance, which will be very similar for all of your wedge swings.

- Start with a square stance. Then, the closer you are to the hole, the narrower your stance should be to promote a more descending blow. It is also advisable to open your stance, as you get closer to the hole, to help add loft to your shots.

- On all your shots, flare you lead foot.

- Ball position can vary depending on the type of shot you are attempting: (1) on a high shot, position the ball slightly forward of center, (2) on a regular shot, position the ball in the middle of your stance, and (3) on a low running shot, position the ball slightly back of center.

- Here's where is gets interesting. In the Pelz 3x4 System, you swing your hands back to 7:30 on a ¼ back-swing (butt of club pointing in front of ball), to 9:00 on a ½ back-swing (butt of club pointing straight down toward ground), and to 10:30 on a ¾ back-swing (butt pointing away from ball). Remember that in a pitch shot, you should NEVER take a full swing because balance and accuracy always outweigh power and distance.

- On the down-swing you should feel as though you arms are glued to your upper chest and be sure to turn your chest towards the target. This is a real key. You will not be consistent, especially under pressure, if you strike your pitches with just your arms and hands. The speed at which you turn through impact will determine the distance of your shot.

- Keep you lower body still. If you rise up on your toes on a full shot back-swing, keep your feet planted with your wedges.

- Your follow through will also determine the length and height of your shots. To propel the ball lower and longer (i.e. a back pin position), cut your follow through and swing to just above belt level. This will allow the ball to release back to the pin. To propel to ball higher and shorter (i.e. a front pin position), allow your follow through to go up and past your head.

To Review – on the back-swing (a) keep your front foot planted and (b) abbreviate your arm swing. On the down-swing, (a) keep your lower body quiet and (b) rotate your upper body (chest) towards the target after impact.

With the 3x4 System, you need to spend some time gauging the distances you propel the ball with each wedge and each swing. You could do this over 4 weekends by taking one wedge and gauging the distance you propel the ball with the four swings as part of your warm up routine before a round. Then write down the distances on a small slip of paper and tape them to the shaft of your wedge for easy reference. If you find that you have neither the time nor the patience to measure the various distances specified in #9 above, use just one swing – the 9:00 or ½ swing. The key is to make sure the butt of your club points straight down to the ground on your back-swing. Never higher. Accelerating the club's speed through impact will give you consistent distances. A good checkpoint routine is to utilize the Mike Weir – Karrie Webb Waggle. Swing your club to the 9:00 or ½ back-swing position and quickly look at where your hands are and whether or not the butt of the club is pointing straight down to the ground. Then, just return the club to the address position and restart you swing without further delay. It's that simple. One swing and one position for your back-swing. Feel it and repeat it, because this, my friend, will become your favorite money shot.

Intrinsic Golf Basic Swing Development exercises 10.7 – 10.9 and 10.10 – 10.12 on the following page will help you find, feel and ingrain your pitching motion.

Figure 10.7

Figure 10.8

Figure 10.9

Figure 10.10

Figure 10.11

Figure 10.12

6. TROUBLE SHOTS AND UNEVEN LIES

Heavy Rough – Swinging out of the heavy rough is a lot like swinging out of a fairway bunker since your goal is exactly the same – *Get out of it!* Pick a club that will give you the greatest margin for error. Do not try a career shot or something you saw Tiger do on TV. Here are four simple suggestions that will help you reach your goal.

- Open the clubface a little at address to allow for the tendency of the grass to close the clubface during the swing.

- Grip the club firmer than usual to also keep the clubface from closing during the swing.

- Play the ball slightly in back of the bottom of your swing arc to ensure a sharper down-swing angle.

Allow for the fact that the ball will roll more once it comes out of the rough because it will typically be "hot" off the clubface and then just swing. Do not try to power the ball on to the green – that's when double and triple bogeys occur.

Again, your goal is to get out of the rough. Don't try to overpower the shot and possibly hurt yourself or try a shot that has a good chance of leaving your ball in the rough. Just swing the club and accelerate through impact and you'll get out of trouble in one shot.

Uphill, Downhill and Sidehill Lies – When dealing with real estate, the three most important criteria are location, location, and location! When dealing with uneven lies, the three most important criteria are balance, balance and balance! As stated earlier, before every shot in Intrinsic Golf we take three practice swings. By doing this, we constantly validate our swing. We feel our swing for this specific shot and we practice our tempo and balance for this specific set of conditions.

- On an Uphill lie, it is inevitable that you will leave more weight than normal on you rear leg as you swing. Because of this the tendency is to pull or hook your shots. Therefore you should adjust for this by aligning yourself to the right of your target.

Additionally, because you are hitting uphill you will be increasing the loft on the club. So choose a club that is stronger than you would normally use for that distance (for a 9 iron shot, use an 8 or 7 iron). Now, just swing the club and maintain your balance.

- On a Downhill lie, it is inevitable that you will leave more weight than normal on your front leg as you swing. Because of this the tendency is to push or slice you shots. Therefore you should align yourself to the left of your target. Additionally, because you are hitting downhill you will be decreasing the loft on the club. So choose a club that is weaker that you would normally use for the distance (for a 7 iron shot, use an 8 or 9 iron). Again, just swing your club and maintain your balance. Also, on downhill lies you might consider opening your stance slightly to help release your front side towards to hole. If you fall forward after swinging through contact – don't worry about it!

- On Sidehill lies, it is important to put more weight on your heels when the ball is below your feet and expect the ball to travel from left to right (assumes right handed players). When the ball is above your feet, put more weight on the balls of your feet and expect the ball to travel from right to left (again, assumes right handed players). On both shots, take a smooth, leisurely swing with just your upper body and use a stronger club to compensate for the loss of distance.

Again, take your three practice swings in order to gauge your proper ball position, to practice your tempo and to ensure that your swing is *balanced, balanced, balanced!*

The Trouble Shot – Finally there is one more shot that will help you lower your score and that is what we call the 150-yard under the tree limb shot. The goal here is to advance the ball without getting into further trouble. This shot won't work if you have to carry the ball in the air 30 yards or more. This shot is your – long grounder. Take three 9:00 to 3:00 practice swings to determine the bottom of your swing arc and position the ball back in your stance. Keep your stance wide to ensure a flat swing and using just your arms – *do not cock your wrists* – bring the club back so your arms and shaft are almost parallel at the 9 o'clock position. Keeping your arms firm and your head still, swing the club with a dead arm motion accelerating through impact until your arms again are straight with the shaft at the 3 o'clock position. Hold the follow through pointing at the target. You will hit a low hard grounder that will get you back on the fairway or close to the green. A Fairway wood is a better choice for this shot than a long iron because it has a wider sole to slide into the ball in case you hit the shot fat.

Intrinsic Golf's Basic Swing Development exercises 10.10 to 10.12 will help you find and ingrain the feel for Uneven Lie shots and exercises 10.7 to 10.9 will help you with the feel for Trouble Shots.

Figure 10.10

Figure 10.11

Figure 10.12

Figure 10.7

Figure 10.8

Figure 10.9

7. YOUR CALL – DRAW OR FADE THE BALL

When you are under pressure and shot consistency is a must, it is comforting to know that your **Intrinsic Golf** swing can produce a repeatable right to left (draw) or left to right (fade) golf shot (wedges will go straight, but all other clubs will produce shots with a specific direction tendency).

At **Intrinsic Golf** we believe strongly in developing a consistent, repeatable ball flight because it's easier to maintain, especially off the tee (using almost any club). To accomplish this, your goal should be to eliminate one side of the fairway, thereby giving you the best chance of propelling the ball into the short grass (see the following 40-yard-wide fairway examples).

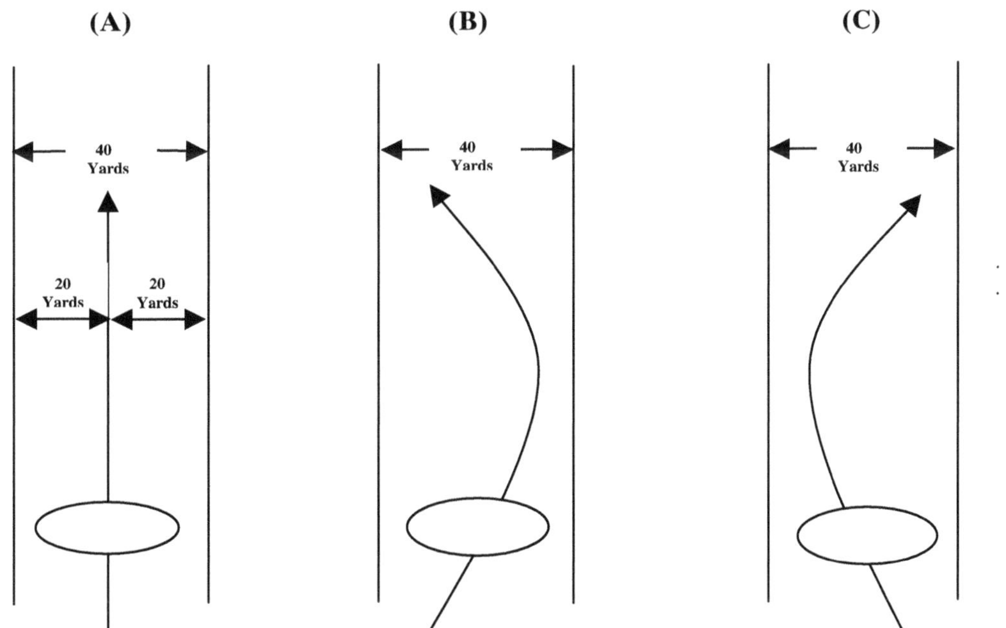

(A) Straight Shot – The toughest shot to hit in the fairway because you only have a 20-yard margin of error to work with. If you make a mistake, either right or left, you can easily end up in the rough.

(B) Draw – Eliminates the right side and gives you 40-yards of error margin on the left.

(C) Fade – Eliminates the left side and gives you 40-yards of error margin on the right.

To produce a draw, first strengthen your grip (both V's pointing to right shoulder) and grip the club loosely in both hands. Second, change your address position by setting your feet, hips, and shoulders, as well as the clubface, square to the target. Next, determine ball position by taking three practice swings and then position the ball slightly back in your stance from your normal ball position. Now slide your rear foot backwards slightly while flaring it out until your hips and shoulders are pointing slightly right of the target (R.H. golfers). Ball flight will give you feedback on how far back you should slide and flare your back foot. Finally, swing along your shoulder and hip lines, while keeping your rear foot grounded to allow the clubface to rollover through the impact area. Your arms, not your hands, should control the rollover. Again, ball flight feedback will tell you how much you should roll your arms closed. A good mental image to help you with this is one where you are rotating your upper body to the left while up ending a bucket of water as you move to the left. After impact, the back of your left wrist (R.H. golfers) should be pointing down toward the ground. You will note that a draw requires a flatter more rounded swing arc or plane.

To produce a fade, first weaken you grip (both V's pointing to your nose) and grip the club tighter so it won't roll over during impact. Second, change your address position by setting your feet, hips, shoulders, and the clubface square to the target. Next, determine your ball position by taking three practice swings and then position the ball slightly forward from you normal ball position. Now flare your front foot open and point your back foot towards the ball until your hips and shoulders are aimed slightly left of target (R.H. golfers). Ball flight will give you feedback on how far you should flare your front foot open. Then just swing along your shoulder and hip lines, holding the clubface open through impact. As before, ball flight feedback will tell you if you are releasing the club instead of holding the face open. A good mental image is to again visualize the bucket of water. Swing the bucket down and spill the water toward your right side. After impact, your left wrist (R.H. golfers) should be pointed upwards. You will note that a fade requires a more upright swing and a higher arm finish.

A couple of final comments – woods, long irons and mid-irons, because of their straighter faces and lack of loft, will draw or fade a ball easier than lofted clubs like wedges. Also, a draw will travel farther than a fade. So when playing a draw, use one club weaker than normal and when playing a fade, use one club stronger than normal.

Intrinsic Golf Basic Swing Development Exercises 10.7 to 10.9 and 10.10 to 10.12 will help you find, feel and ingrain these shots.

Figure 10.7

Figure 10.8

Figure 10.9

Figure 10.10

Figure 10.11

Figure 10.12

8. PRACTICE SWINGS, POSTURE, AIM AND FIRE

My good friend and co-author of **Intrinsic Golf** related the following to me. While sitting on his back porch, which faces the 7th fairway of the golf course he lives on, he has observed numerous golfers who jump out of their cart, grab a club, walk over to their ball and, without taking proper aim or even one practice swing, proceed to hit their ball into the nearby trees or houses. Then they jump back into their cart and drive off down the fairway muttering unprintable phrases! What did they expect – a miracle?

Even though we believe strongly in playing the game by feel and without confusing swing thoughts, we do not recommend trying to advance the ball without at least getting into the proper posture and taking a few practice swings. In fact, we believe you should always pick out your target, set up properly, take your three practice swings, address the ball appropriately, *and then swing without utilizing any mechanical thoughts.* These basic elements make up your pre-shot setup routine, which is not part of your swing.

The setup, which is composed of spine angle, posture, aim and grip, is even more important than your personal **Intrinsic Golf** swing. Why, because everything in your swing reacts to it. If you are set up poorly, then even with a perfect swing, the ball will not go towards the target. Conversely, once you are setup properly, you can begin your swing and fire at the target with confidence.

Here are some valuable suggestions on properly setting up for a shot.

- *Don't ever try to advance the ball without first taking a few practice swings!* Yes, we said swings! Remember, as stated earlier in the first section, your pre-shot routine should include taking three practice swings before each shot. This will enable you to gauge your proper ball position, practice your tempo and ensure that your swing is both repeatable and balanced. Additionally, these three swings will keep your **Intrinsic Golf** swing grooved and guarantee consistency of your path towards the target.

- *Get into the proper posture.* This is the one area that most mid- to high-handicappers fail to recognize as the major cause of swing inconsistencies. The cure is simple – *bend to one side and bend forward.*

The reason for side and forward bending is to put you into the best athletic address position to propel a ball towards a target. Side bending moves your center of gravity either forward of or behind the ball to promote the proper weight shift to your front foot on wedge shots and short irons or to your back foot on full shots. Start by standing straight up and hanging a club straight down from the middle of your chest. Then, holding the club firmly against your chest, tilt your body to either the right until the shaft points to your left instep (full shots) or to the left until the shaft points to your right instep (wedge and short irons shots).

Many golfers tend to set up with their spine too centered, which can lead to either a poor turn or a reverse weight shift. Being too centered produces a swing that moves out and away from the target on the down-swing, making the club bottom out too early and causing you to hit across the ball or hit fat or thin shots.

Thanks to an article by Tom Stickney II in the December 1999 issue of Golf Magazine, we can compare the side and forward bending of Professional Golfers to those of 5-, 15-, and 25-handicappers. Here's the comparison –

- Touring Pros bend 8 to 9 degrees away from or towards the target and forward 33 to 34 degrees from the hip sockets.

- 5-Handicappers bend 5 to 8 degrees away from or towards the target and forward 29 to 33 degrees from the hip sockets.

- 15-Handicappers bend 2 to 5 degrees away from or towards the target and forward 28 to 32 from the hip sockets.

- 25-Handicappers bend 0 to 2 degrees away from or towards the target and forward 22 to 26 from the hip sockets.

Bending forward, as stated earlier, puts you into a more athletic position to propel the ball towards the target and it keeps your swing plane and path grooved. When you do both correctly, the laws of physics will work with your body to provide maximum support to your swing, thus enabling you to move the club through impact at a higher rate of speed. More speed means more distance and, if your path is consistent, the result will be straighter shots.

Start by walking-in and adjusting your feet to achieve your normal stance. Now bend your knees slightly and start bending forward until your weight is over the balls of your feet. If your weight is on your heels, your center of gravity is too far back. Your arms should hang straight down and not rest on your chest. To gain consistency in your **Intrinsic Golf** swing, make it a point to always bend towards or away from your target first and then bend over. This will result in longer, straighter shots, which will take your game to a higher level.

Another thing you must incorporate into your set up routine is to aim your shot. According to Jack Nicklaus (Jack Nicklaus' Lesson Tee with Ken Bowden, Fireside Books, 1978), "Don't aim at a fairway or green, aim at a spot in the fairway or at a portion of the green."

Start by picking out your target. Stand behind the ball and visualize an imaginary path between your ball and the target (fairway or pin) then pick out an intermediate target on that path like a divot, leaf or spot of discolored grass about three feet in front of the ball. Aim your clubface at this nearby target rather than at the one in the distance. Now walk to your address position and walk into your stance, lowering the club to a hovering position just above the ground. Aim the clubface down the target line and make sure your feet, knees, hips, shoulders are in line left, right or square to the target (fade, draw, or straight shot).

Next, bend forward over the ball and bend your knees slightly. Now bend to the appropriate side to create the correct tilt at address. Remember, more swings are inconsistent due to centered spines than by any other set-up flaw. Now complete the routine by taking a waggle or two with the club to relax (swing thoughts creep in if you stand over the ball for more than five seconds) and then FIRE at your target.

Additional keys to a successful set up:

- ➢ The squareness of your body, especially your shoulders, is another key to a consistent swing path. The hands and arms swing the club. They both hang down from the shoulders, so it makes sense that the arms and club go where the shoulders go. Since most high handicappers naturally hit the ball from left to right (slice), the more they open their shoulders (align them left of parallel), the more they will cut across the ball. Therefore, square to slightly closed shoulders (aligned slightly right of parallel) are a must to assure a consistent in to out swing path.

- A technique that will help make sure your feet are aligned parallel left of the target line (R.H. golfers) is to extend both of your arms parallel in front of you while standing behind the ball. Your right arm should extend through the ball and at the target, establishing your target line. Your left arm should be parallel (as if it were the second rail of a train track) indicating your stance line. If you want to hit a draw, your stance line (left arm) would be in line with the pin and your target line (right arm) would also be in line with the pin. If you hit a fade, your target line can be left of the pin and your stance line even farther left.

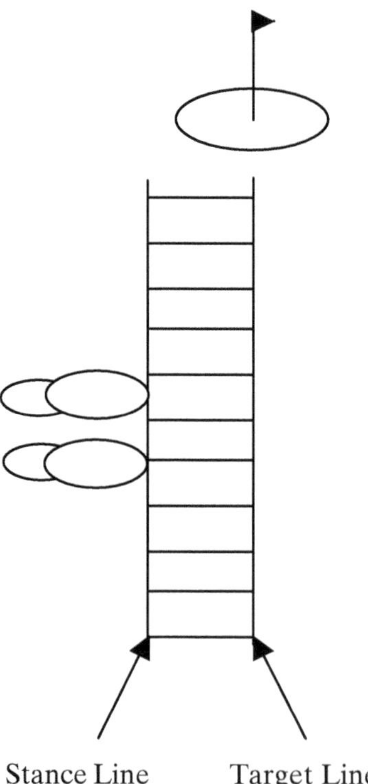

SECTION 3 – PRACTICE AND EVALUATION

"Practice doesn't make perfect, it's perfect practice that makes perfect. In fact, the more I do practice, the luckier I get."[8]

Gary Player

[8] From Golf Begins at 50 by Gary Player with Desmond Tolhurst.

1. THE ONE DAY PRACTICE AT THE RANGE

As indicated earlier, this book was written to help golfers who would like to improve their game but do not have sufficient time to practice or take lessons. If this describes your situation, I'm sure you will agree that even busy people like you occasionally have a day when you would like to play some golf but can't put together a foursome and don't feel like playing as a single. This is when spending an equal amount of time at the range might strike your fancy. Here's how we at **Intrinsic Golf** recommend you spend that time in order to gain the most benefit.

Start your swing development practice session from the hole and work backwards towards the tee. Begin with putting and focus on *grip, stance, feel, and stroke.*

Putting – 30 minutes followed by a 10-minute break:

A. **Grip** – Hold the putter in your palms with both thumbs pointing straight down the shaft. Your grip pressure should be loose.
B. **Stance** – Your shoulders, forearms, hips, knees and feet should be in a straight line parallel to the target line. Your eyes should be either over the ball or slightly inside the target line.
C. **Ball Position** – Position your body so the ball is one to two inches in front of the low point of your stroke.
D. **Stroke** – Swing straight back and straight through or optionally in a slightly inside back to square and then slightly inside forward arc. Hold your finish.
E. **Five Drills You Can Use:**
    1. *25 in a row, 3-foot Putting Drill* – Keep hitting 3-foot putts until you make 25 in a row.
    2. *The Ladder Distance Putting Drill* – Place tees 3', 6', 10', 15', and 20' from the cup. Stroke several putts from each distance, using only one ball. That way you are not just standing over the putts – hitting one after another – you are focusing on your grip, setup, ball position and stroke each time. Always take 3 practice strokes before hitting each putt.
    3. *Around the World Drill* – Place 12 balls in a circle around the hole, with each ball being 6' from the hole. Take 3 practice strokes and then putt each ball into the hole.

4. *Four Corners Drill* – Place 4 balls 3', 6', 9' and 12' from the hole in the North, South, East, and West directions. Take 3 practice strokes and then putt each of the balls into the hole.
5. *Safety Draw Back Drill* – Place a ball at least 20' from the cup. Take 3 practice strokes then stroke the putt towards the hole. If you miss, move the ball back one putter length from the hole and, after 3 practice strokes, stroke the putt into the cup. This drawback allows you to work on lag putting those dreaded 3-4 foot par or bogey putts. Putting alone can represent anywhere from 40 to 50 percent of your score – therefore no area of practice can lower your score quicker than putting.

Chipping – focus on *grip, stance, feel, and stroke* – 30 minutes followed by a 10-minute break.

1. **Grip** – Choke up and utilize a neutral grip with both V's pointing towards your chin.
2. **Stance** – Feet together in a slightly open stance with both feet flared. 65% or your weight should be over your front foot to ensure a more descending blow. Hands should be well ahead of ball position with butt of club pointing towards left hip.
3. **Ball Position** – depending on the shot, the ball position should be from the middle of your stance back to just outside your right ankle. *Never forward.*
4. **Stroke** - you can either use a putting stroke or one that has a slight hinge in your right wrist. With both of these strokes, it's paramount not to break your left wrist at impact trying to scoop the ball. Finish with both hands past your legs and hold that position for five seconds.
5. **Experiment** – use various lofted clubs (6-iron to SW) to see how different lofts affect both carry and roll and experiment with different lies around the green.

Sand Play – focus on grip, stance, feel, and swing, as well as getting the ball on the green within six feet of the cup – 30 minutes followed by a 10-minute break.

1. **Grip** – grip the club in a neutral grip with both V's pointing towards your chin.
2. **Stance** – lead foot should be flared to the left and the back foot should be pointed towards the ball. Aim your shoulders slightly left

of the pin. 65% of your weight should be over your front foot and the clubface should be aimed directly at the target.

3. **Ball Position** – position the ball at least two inches in front of lowest point of the swing, but not past the inside of your front ankle.
4. **Swing** – use a ¾ back-swing and accelerate on the down-swing. Enter the sand 1" to 2" behind the ball and *don't quit on the swing.* Allow your hands to swing up and above your shoulders. An incomplete follow-through is the number one problem in poor bunker play. Swing should be along your shoulder line.
5. **Experiment** – try various shot lengths and lies (buried, up-slope, down-slope, etc.).

Lunch Break – 30 minutes maximum – you don't want to stiffen-up or get lethargic from eating a complete meal. On the other hand, you do want to rest your body and replenish your loss of fluids.

Wedge Play – focus on *grip, stance, feel, and swing, as well as distance control* – 30 minutes followed by a 10-minute break.

1. **Grip** – use your full-swing grip (both V's pointed in the same direction). Experiment (choke-up on the grip) to create different club lengths and various length back-swings.
2. **Stance** – flare your lead foot, and square your rear foot.
3. **Ball Position** – ball should be in the middle of your stance, but experiment with ball position from two inches forward to two inches back of middle to gauge distance and trajectory.
4. **Swing** – (have some fun) try ¼ length back-swing, with ball centered, forward and then back. Try ½ length back-swing, with ball centered, forward and then back. Finally, try ¾ length back-swing, with ball centered, forward and then back. Calculate your distances. You need to know how far you hit the ball with each swing.
5. **Experiment** – use all of your wedges with various length back-swings – these are your money shots.

The closer you get your wedge shots to the pin, the better your putting will become. These are the shots you must master. Practicing them will also help your timing, tempo and feel. Don't machine-gun your shots. Use multiple targets and move your target and your selection of club around. Try different length back-swings. Practicing your wedge shots so that you hit the ball closer to the pin, along with improved putting, is guaranteed to lower your scores.

Irons – short, mid and long – 30 minutes with 10-minute break.

1. **Grip** – use your full-swing grip (both V's pointing in the same direction). Concentrate on holding the club more in the palm of your left hand and in the fingers of your right hand.
2. **Stance** – use your natural walk-in stance. Flare your foot/feet if necessary and square your stance or close it depending on the posture and ball flight you desire. The butt of the club should be pointing towards your left thigh on short iron shots and gradually towards center, as the irons get longer. However, the butt of the club should never pass your belly-button. Make sure you bend your spine away or towards the target and bend forward at the hips as discussed earlier.
3. **Ball Position** – position the ball one ball forward of the lowest point of your swing. Then move the ball one ball backwards of the lowest point of your swing. Observe the difference in results.
4. **Swing** – Concentrate on tempo, balance and acceleration through impact and take dead aim at your target on all your swings. Remember to take your three practices swings before each shot. Hold your follow through at the finish. Feel every part of your swing and focus on accuracy, not distance. Using your mid and long irons, try to work the ball right to left (draw) and left to right (fade) and employ your four-syllable cadence to ingrain your swing tempo.

Woods – Driver and Fairway – focus on *accuracy (not length), and on grip, stance, feel, tempo, and swing* – 30 minutes to finish.

1. **Grip** – again, use your full swing grip (both V's pointing in the same direction). As with your irons, concentrate on holding the shaft more in the palm of you left hand and in the fingers of your right hand. Employ a loose grip to provide a better release for a draw and tighten your grip to produce a fade.
2. **Stance** – pay attention to your feet first. Do I flare my back foot and drop it back to get a bigger turn? Do I close my front foot to provide more of a brace to swing against?
3. **Ball Position** – position the ball one to two balls forward of the lowest point of your swing. Be very precise with respect to ball position when using these longer clubs. A small variance can cause a change in your swing path through impact that might result in a miss-hit shot.

4. **Swing** – don't over-swing – concentrate on accuracy, not power. Focus on tempo, balance, and acceleration through impact. Remember to take three practice swings before each shot. Always pick a target and align yourself parallel to the target line. Finish with five drives that would land in the fairway of the first hole of your favorite course. Hold your finish. Remember, you can only swing as hard as your intrinsic swing will allow. Any harder and it becomes a hit.

Listed below are some helpful thoughts about swinging. Use/visualize them where appropriate to help you ingrain the feel of your personal swing while practicing on the range:

- To and Fro
- Back and Forth
- Side to Side
- Inhale – Exhale
- Pendulum Clock
- Child Swinging on a Swing.
- Branches Swaying in the Breeze.
- Hands move the clubhead back in the back-swing – Arms swing the clubhead forward on the down-swing.
- Weight shift, turn back and cock – weight shift, turn through and re-cock.
- A swing is a series of circular motions without any individual parts.

If you practice as suggested, this day at the range will have lasted about 4 hours and 20 minutes – very similar to what a round of golf would require. However, in this case you will have stroked (putts), chipped, pitched and swung your short, mid and long irons, as well as your driver, several hundred times. If you schedule this outing at the range just once a year, you will be amazed at the improvement you will experience in your golf game.

One final tip – While you are practicing, take careful notes on how far you hit each club (a rangefinder will come in handy here). For Irons and Wedges, you are looking of air-carry only. However, with Wedges you have to consider both half and full shot distances. With Woods, include both air-carry and roll when recording distances. Write down the distances on a card and carry it with you on the course. Or, if you prefer, tape a small slip of paper with the distance for each club to the shaft of each club. Knowing the precise distance each club is likely to travel will be extremely helpful in choosing the right club in the distance control part of your game.

2. A BAKER'S DOZEN OF DRILLS YOU CAN DO AT HOME

Okay, if you really, really don't have the time to go to the range, but you are willing to practice if you don't have to go anywhere, here are a number of drills you can do without leaving home. Some are best done inside, some outside, but all of them can be done on your property.

1. **Practice Gripping a Training Grip** – Buy a training grip and place it on an old club (yard sales and pro shop used club barrels are excellent places to look) that you cut down to about 30 inches or less. Then, while you are watching TV, put the clicker down and grip the club. Soon you will be able to find your correct grip by feel – with your eyes closed! The grip is your only connection to the club and most ball flight mistakes, even with a good swing and swing-path, are cause by a poor grip.

2. **Tap Drill** – This drill helps enhance your feel and hand-wrist dexterity! Hold a club by the club head in each hand and point the grips down and away from you – towards the floor. Tap the ends together as you extend your arms and hands out to the side. You will soon notice that as you soften your grip and allow more feel to take over, the easier it gets. Observe and feel the grip pressure in you hands and the flexibility of your wrists while doing this drill. Stiff wrists and arms along with tight grip pressure may give you the impression of control at first – but in the end looseness and soft pressure provide the answer.

3. **The Hitchhike and Double Hitchhike Drills** – Put your club aside, place your right hand behind your back and assume an imaginary address position with your left arm. Now turn back and swing your left arm back and up until your thumb touches your right shoulder. Then swing your arm back down and through until your thumb touches your left shoulder on the follow through. Do it over and over until you can feel a natural rhythmic motion that emphasizes bicep curls with your left arm at both ends of your swing. Now exchange arms and place your left arm behind you and do this drill with your right thumb touching each shoulder. Again, you should feel a natural, rhythmic motion that emphasizes bicep curls at both ends of your swing with your right thumb. Finally, place your hands together and swing both arms up and back concentrating on the

bicep curls. First in your back-swing and then down and through to your follow-through position. These drills will allow you to feel a natural, rhythmic swing with both arms separated, then together, emphasizing the bicep curl cocking position.

4. **Hands Release Drill** – This drill allows you to practice the proper hand and wrist action during the "release" point of your swing. Start by placing your hands in front of you and towards your right side so that your left palm is facing away from you. Flip them over as fast as you can and then add a slight swinging motion. You will start to feel and understand why tight grip pressure decreases, not increases club head speed. Stiff hands and wrists are slow hands and wrists. Soft hands and wrists are quick hands and wrists. Remember in Intrinsic Golf, we are replacing Power with Speed, therefore, "loose grips equals faster rips."

5. **The Horizontal Release Drill** – Hold the club straight out in front of you, then swing it back until the face of the club points to the sky and your right arm is bicep curled. Now swing the club forward and through, rolling you arms and wrists over so your forearms touch and the face of the club points to the ground. This drill teaches you to feel the release of your hands through impact instead of blocking the ball with stiff hands and wrists. You can use your 30' club and do this drill indoors.

6. **Balance Drill** – Do this on the lawn or at least in an area where you have cleared out the furniture. Close your eyes and swing a club (a wedge will do fine). Swing it slowly at first, feeling all the individual parts of your swing motion. Then begin to increase your speed while you maintain your balance. What you will begin to feel is that your optimum swing speed, *with balance*, is not as fast as you may have thought – even though you are currently using that faster speed on the course. Most touring professionals say they swing at about 85% of the swing speed they are capable of reaching.

7. **Prop Drill** – Hold the end of a long club vertical with your left hand out in front of you and rest the opposite end of the club on the ground slightly behind the center of your stance. Now, swing a choked-up wedge down and under your left arm like you are hitting a ball positioned under your arm. Feel how your feet move forward and push forward and how your back shoulder moves down and

under on the down-swing. Also, feel your right hand release the club with your head behind where the ball would be.

8. **The Quarterback Drill** – Get a Football and emulate a quarterback's stance when he's receiving the snap from center. Your spine should be straight, not hunched or curled. Your weight should be on the balls of your feet and your head should be up. This mimics the same athletic position you should be in when you address the golf ball. There is only one difference, you should tilt backward or forward along the target line as discussed earlier, depending on whether you want to mimic a wedge or full shot.

9. **The One-Two-Three Back Swing Drill** – Start at your normal address position with the butt of club facing towards left thigh. Bring the club up so that your shaft rests on your right shoulder. Now, while maintaining your posture, turn as far as you can to your right and raise your hands to the cocked position. You are now in your own personal back-swing position. Look at you hands, feel you feet, posture, and weight distribution over your right foot. Hold this position for five seconds.

10. **The Four-Five-Six Follow Through Drill** – Start at your normal address position with the butt of club pointing towards your left hip. Bring the club up so that the shaft rests on your left shoulder. Now, while maintaining your posture, turn as far as your can to your left and raise your hands to the cocked position. You are now in your own personal follow-through position. Your body should have turned toward the target. Look at your hands, feel your feet, posture, and weight distribution over your left foot. Hold this position for five seconds.

11. **Putting Drills** – (A) *Straight Putts*: If you don't have an indoor cup, cut a cup-sized hole out of some thin plastic and place it on the floor. Pace off 3', 6' and 9' distances and practice your putting. Make 25 in a row from 3', 10 in a row from 6' and 50% of your putts from 9'. (B) *Safety Draw Back*: Start 10 feet from cup and stroke 25 putts toward the hole. On any putt that would not have been made, move away from the cup one putter length and then stroke a second putt.

12. **Chipping Drills** – Move back as far away from your indoor cup as you have available space. Use only you highest lofted club(s) (LW or SW) and practice chipping the plastic balls into the cup.

13. **Whiffle Ball Drills – Indoors or Outdoors** – (A) *Indoors:* Get a wastebasket or clothesbasket and practice chipping/pitching balls into them at different distances. You can try putting the basket behind a chair or couch and pitch balls into the basket. Be creative, but don't use "I can't get outside" as an excuse not to practice chipping. (B) *Outdoors:* Find a clothesline or bush that runs parallel to the ground at eye level. Start at about 10 yards away and lob some balls over the object. It should be pretty easy. Then move forward and see how close you can get to the object and still get over it. This drill teaches you that the closer you get to an object, the more you have to open your stance and clubface to get the ball over the object.

Please remember that these drills do not replace the daily **Intrinsic Golf Basic Swing Development Program** exercises. These drills are an addition to those exercises, which take only two minutes a day to do.

3. THE INTRINSIC GOLF REPORT CARD

The Intrinsic Golf Report Card is a personal worksheet that allows you to chart your play so that you can pinpoint both your weaknesses and your strengths. Most golfers, believe it or not, do not really know what areas of their game need improvement. As a result, they spend far too much time working on their strengths – thus improvement is typically slight or non-existent.

Make photocopies of the following worksheet and fill one out during each round. Analyze the totals in each category to identify your weak areas and then practice shots at the range that will strengthen them. Or, if you really don't have the time to practice at the range, incorporate some time into your warm-up routine before each round to work on these weak areas.

Intrinsic Golf Report Card

Hole #	1	2	3	4	5	6	7	8	9	10	11	12	13	14	15	16	17	18	Total	Notes
Par																				
Distance																				
Score																				
Fairways Hit																				
Greens in Regulation																				
Sand Saves																				
Up and Down (Around Green)																				
Up and Down (From Fairway)																				
Total Putts																				
Mulligans																				
3-Putts																				

Course: ________________ Date: ________________

SECTION 4 – THE EQUIPMENT

"No matter how new, pricey, high tech, or great-looking your clubs are, they won't help you score better if they are not right for the way you play."[9]

Hank Haney

[9] From The Only Golf Lesson You'll Ever Need by Hank Haney and John Huggan.

1. BUY A BETTER GAME WITH PROPERLY FITTED CLUBS

If you were wondering whether or not we at **Intrinsic Golf** believe that today's newer equipment can improve your game – the answer is *YES*!

I once bought a new car and I will never forget what the salesman said to me that day. He told me he had a big selection of cars on the lot, but if I would let him, he would build a car especially for me, with the style, color and all the amenities I would like to have. It would be built specifically for me. I liked the idea of owning a car that met my requirements exactly.

I feel that same way about golf equipment. I don't want to buy a set of golf clubs off the rack. I want a set of custom-fitted golf clubs that (1) I like to look at, and (2) have all the characteristics to compliment and ensure that I get the most out of my swing. You shouldn't care what clubs Tiger, Jack, Phil or Sergio use. You should only care about what kind of clubs will best fit you and your personal **Intrinsic Golf** swing.

Continuing with the car analogy, let's look at the engine. You wouldn't put a 4-cylinder engine is a Mercedes 600, would you? Of course you wouldn't, because the Mercedes would not perform properly. Likewise, you must be careful of your golf club engine or you too will experience poor performance. The golf club's engine is the shaft. There are four things you must consider with regards to the shaft: (1) flex, (2) length, (3) weight, and (4) material (steel, graphite, or composite). The most important of these characteristics is flex. To swing a club correctly, the shaft must feel a little whippy. So, if you choose the correct shaft, it should be on the soft side. Again, because you are swinging the club and not hitting at the ball, it's important to let the club do some of the work for you. While a stiff shaft definitely favors a hitter, in a lot of cases tip stiffness will give you the ball flight you are looking for (flexible tip – more height, stiff tip – lower ball flight).

The second most important characteristic is length. Swing the longest driver you can control and propel the ball into the fairway. The reason is simple. The longer the club, the longer the swing arc and the faster the club head speed will be with your personal **Intrinsic Golf** swing. And, of course, the faster your club head speed, the more distance you will achieve. However, for irons and wedges stick to more conventional lengths (1/2" to 1" longer than standard), because accuracy is much more important than distance.

The third and fourth most important club characteristics are weight and shaft material. Graphite and lightweight steel top the list in both categories. Particularly with longer shafts, lightness and flexibility are important factors. Both compliment and contribute to added speed, because you can swing a lighter club faster. There may be a 40-gram difference in the weight between a steel-shafted wood and one made using a graphite shaft. As with increased shaft flexibility, lighter shaft weight will let the club do some of the speed work for you. We recommend graphite shafts as the number one choice for both reduced weight and increased flexibility.

Now let's address Club Set Makeup – The changes in this area over the last ten years have been dramatic. A larger selection of wedges, as well as more fairway woods and utility clubs in all shapes and sizes are now finding their way into player's bags. Here are some thoughts and suggestions concerning these equipment options:

➢ Drivers – Unless you always play on flat, hard fairways with no hazards, it is not the distance you hit the golf ball (in-the-air carry plus roll), it's carry alone that's most important. How far you can hit the ball in the air over a hazard (i.e. sand, waste area or water hazard) is the question, and a 10.5° to 13° driver with the correct shaft flexibility is most likely the answer.

➢ Fairway woods – You need height to stop a long shot on the green. Therefore, it probably will not improve your score to run out and purchase a 12.5° (strong) fairway wood that will propel your ball closer to the hole, but will seldom if ever stop it on the green. Now you might ask, what's wrong with being closer to the hole even if the ball is off the green? Nothing, if you have a great short game. However, if chipping the ball to the hole from the fringe is not your strength (statistics tells us that 80% of all bogey shots are made close to the green), then laying back to a distance where you can hit a full wedge shot will have a higher probability of getting you closer to the hole. For this reason, your best bet is to choose a 15° 3-wood. Then there are the 4- and 5-woods, in the 16 to 19 degree range, that will give you the height you need to stop the ball on the green – these are the clubs that replace the old 1- and 2-irons. These are also great clubs to use off the tee on tight driving holes. Here's where today's utility clubs make sense, since they can easily replace your 2-, 3- and/or 4-irons. In fact, there are now 3 through PW hybrid irons/woods that can replace almost every iron in your bag.

- Utility Clubs – Some simple rules of thumb concerning these clubs are... If you can't hit a 3-iron 190 yards in the air, put a 7-wood or a 22° utility wood in your bag. If you can't hit a 4-iron 175 yards in the air, put a 9- wood or a 24° utility club in your bag. And, if you can't hit a 5-iron 160 yards in the air, put an 11 wood or a 27° utility club in your bag. Don't look at what the PGA Tour Players have in their bags, look at what the Champion's Tour and LPGA players use. Their games are more comparable to those of the weekend golfer. Utility clubs are easier to hit because they are built with forgiveness in mind. Due to their higher loft, extra mass and sand-wedge like skid curvature on the bottom of the club, they help you propel the ball higher, straighter and with less effort than long irons. The skid curvature also helps if you hit behind the ball, allowing you to walk away with a half decent shot. Utility woods usually come in the 17 to 27 degree range. They have less mass and look different than fairway woods, but they accomplish essentially the same task. The difference is literally "in the eye of the beholder." The point is, if you have trouble hitting long irons – get rid of them and put some utility clubs in your bag.

- Mid- to Short-Irons – Concentrate on clubs that are: (1) cavity-backed – they are more forgiving, (2) offset – they give you more time to square the clubface at impact, and (3) custom fitted – built to the correct length, lie, flex and material specifications to match your swing.

- Wedges – Now we move on down to the wedges. Most pros are now carrying 3 wedges; a pitching wedge (PW), a sand wedge (SW) and a lob wedge (LW). Some even carry four wedges with the addition of either an attack wedge or fairway wedge (50 to 53 degrees) or an extra lob wedge (64 degrees). The attack and fairway wedges were designed to fill the gap between the PW and SW when, about 7 years ago, the golf industry decreased the loft of most irons (2-PW). People began to say WOW; I can hit my pitching wedge as far or farther than my old nine iron. Of course they could, because now they were hitting a PW with the loft of the old 9-iron. Dah! Short game guru, Dave Pelz, is most responsible for the 64-degree wedge. It's a great tool around the green if you have time to practice with it and can fit it into your 14-club arsenal. Otherwise, let the pros use it.

To sum it all up – (1) distance through the air (carry) is more important than carry plus roll, unless you play a lot of flat golf courses with few hazards, (2) fairway and utility woods are more forgiving and easier to hit than long irons and (3) a third wedge or lob wedge to hit over bunkers and out of rough around the green would all be great additions to your bag.

How can you determine which clubs would be best for you and your game? Attend a Manufacturer's Demo Days event. More and more golf equipment companies are letting players test their clubs, especially in early spring before the traditional golf season starts. Try all of their clubs, all of their shafts, and as many shaft flexes as possible – and take notes. Your total set can't exceed 14 clubs, 13 plus your putter. So have some fun, swing with your own swing and build a set of clubs that works for you.

An additional characteristic that must be considered when selecting your clubs is lie angle. This is the angle the shaft creates with the ground when the sole of the club is resting squarely on the turf. Lie angle becomes even more of a factor when you use longer clubs in order to gain extra distance. This is because the way the clubface makes contact with the ground determines the direction the ball is launched and the path it travels. Therefore, lie angle typically must be adjusted to complement club length and it will take some lie-board and range work to determine what is right for you.

The shape, depth and direction of your divots can also tell you a great deal about your swing and the lie of your clubs. Deep 'toe divots' mean your clubs are too flat and will propel the ball to the right. Deep 'heel divots' mean your clubs are too upright and will propel the ball to the left. Why the big deal? Well, would you rather use a 5-iron that is two degrees upright and propel your ball 175 yards straight down the fairway or use a 5-iron that is two degrees flat that propels your ball

175 yards forward, but 20 yards to the right? We assume you would prefer the former to the latter. So for lie angle, the rule of thumb should be – increase your lie angle one degree for every ½ inch you lengthen your club over standard. We at **Intrinsic Golf** strongly recommend that when making any adjustments to your clubs, like length and lie, you use a Certified Club Fitter and not just someone who sells clubs.

Another frequently overlooked characteristic is the clubface angle of your woods. Because of the length of your driver and fairway woods and the softer shafts being used today, your club may come into the impact area with a slightly open face. You can determine if this is happening by observing whether or not you are constantly pushing your shots to the right. The cure here is simple – choose woods with a closed face angle. Ball flight will be your final determinate, but drivers can be closed up to 4 degrees and fairway woods up to 2 degrees. Because loft increases with fairway woods and utility clubs, and backspin comes into play, it is not unusual to have your driver club head closed 2 degrees, your 3-wood one degree, and your 5-wood with a square clubface. Again a certified club fitter can assess your ball flight and determine what's best for your personal swing.

Acquiring clubs fitted specifically for your swing will allow you to propel the golf ball longer, straighter and with much less effort. Try it – you will love the results! A little work and experimentation in this area will absolutely improve your swing, your score, and your enjoyment of the game.

However, if after reading this section you are getting ready to have an anxiety attack thinking that all this equipment knowledge will cause you to revert back to focusing on swing mechanics, allow me to put you at ease. Let's return to the car salesmen analogy discussed at the beginning of this section. He sold me on the benefits of building a car to my specifications, both in amenities and performance. He never mentioned a word about teaching me how to drive the car better. In like manner, acquiring a set of custom-fitted clubs will enhance the results of your personal swing without you ever having to think about it.

Oops! I almost forgot. The type of ball you use will also have an impact on the end result of your swing. Unfortunately, the only way to find the right ball for you is to test them in play. Evaluate how they *feel* when you hit them, and then checkout:

- The trajectory, carry, and distance after they land (a distance ball).
- The trajectory plus the spin you get on the greens (a spin ball).
- The results you get around the green – bump and run shots, short pitches and lobs and, of course, how the ball rolls off your putter.

There are no shortcuts to ball selection. It's all trial and error. What the pro's use or what one of the guys in your favorite foursome uses really has no bearing on how a ball will work for you. Experiment and discover the best ball for your game.

Oops again! For the female golfer, manufacturers have begun making clubs designed not just for women – but also for the way women play. Not just shorter and lighter clubs with more flexible able shafts as in the past, but also with design features that focus on launch angle, speed and loft variances that optimize a women's game. These newer clubs have a very low center of gravity to maximize the height of ball flight and are designed with more mass and sole to allow them to slide easier through sand, grass and rough, without requiring a lot of physical strength. After several years of testing, manufacturers finally realized that a lot of women were hitting their woods and irons the same distance. Simply put, women don't hit down on the ball like men do. They tend to sweep the ball off the ground. The problem is a sweep reduces backspin and creates less lift, which when combined with low launch angles, means less distance. So women now have sets of clubs available that are specifically designed with lofts, launch angles, lengths, and weights that may forever change the way women golfers play the game.

In conclusion, when it comes to golf equipment, both men and women players should Go Shopping. Try different clubs, demo different irons, educate yourself on the type of equipment that will best suit your game. Don't get a second opinion – get several. Ladies, check with women pro's and retailers who can give you first hand experience, not word of mouth information. If you are willing to do some shopping, experimenting and information gathering – YOU CAN buy a better game with properly fitted clubs!

Good luck, you are going to love your new Mercedes (oops – golf clubs)!

2. THE WEIGHTED NRG BALL GOLF SWING TRAINER

We at ***Intrinsic Golf*** believe that the fastest way to find, feel, and groove the path of your own personal golf swing is through the use of a weighted swing training device when doing your 30 to 150 swings per day. Throughout this book we have identified this patented weighted swing training device either as the Weighted NRG BALL Golf Swing Trainer, or more succinctly as the NRG BALL. This 4 lb. golf swing trainer, designed and distributed by Sports Training Devices, LLC (www.nrgball.com), is the best product we have found and the one we use to do the ***Intrinsic Golf* Basic Swing Development Program** exercises in Chapter 10. Exercising with this product for as little as two (2) minutes a day does three important things:

- It grooves the Path of the Clubhead by repetitiously and unconsciously channeling your personal intrinsic swing.

- It squares the Angle of the Clubface to ensure longer and straighter shots, which can be further enhanced by adjustments in grip and stance.

- It increases Clubhead Speed through Impact by strengthening your body and increasing your flexibility.

For more information on ***Intrinsic Golf*** or the **Weighted NRG BALL Golf Swing Trainer by Sports Training Devices,** visit us on the World Wide Web at www.intrinsicgolf.com.

iv. AFTERWORD

We hope this book has given you a better understanding of *How to Play Better Golf When You Don't Have Time to Practice or Take Lessons*. The information contained on these pages will help you, if you follow the program closely, find and ingrain your own personal golf swing. You will develop a feel for your personal swing and, if you do the exercises described in the **Intrinsic Golf Basic Swing Development Program**, you will be able to consistently produce a solid swing that allows you to propel the golf ball longer and straighter than you ever have in the past.

We also hope this book has helped convince you that there is no 'single' or 'right' way to swing a golf club. Through education, experimentation, practice and playing your way, you will come to believe, as we do, that swinging the club is better than hitting at the ball and that improving your short game will lower your score quicker and help you maintain those low scores longer, than trying to use power to hit the ball farther. Finally, we hope you now believe in and are committed to finding your own personal swing and playing by feel, which is easier to learn and repeat than trying to learn and play with someone else's methods and mechanics.

Just reading this book will not make you a better player. However, players just like you have proven that following the **Intrinsic Golf** philosophy and exercising as shown in the **Basic Swing Development Program** will make you a better player. Swinging the club with tempo is definitely better than hitting at the ball with power. How do we know? How can we be so sure? Because it's **Intrinsic Golf – *It's Within You*.**

v. ABOUT THE AUTHOR

Bill Denehy is a former Major League Pitcher with the New York Mets, the Washington Senators and the Detroit Tigers. During his career, he played for such notables as Billy Martin and Ted Williams, and the latter taught him a great deal about the art and science of hitting a ball. Bill also coached at the professional and collegiate levels and counts Houston's Jeff Bagwell and New York Yankee Roger Clemens as two of his prize pupils.

After leaving baseball, Bill moved to Orlando, Florida, and focused his attention on improving his golf game. Within a couple years, he reduced his handicap to 4 and became a Certified Instructor with a Top 25 golf school. For the past 8 ½ years Bill has been teaching golf and playing in celebrity tournaments in and around the Central Florida area.

www.ingramcontent.com/pod-product-compliance
Ingram Content Group UK Ltd.
Pitfield, Milton Keynes, MK11 3LW, UK
UKHW051129260726
13967UKWH00010B/2950

9 781412 000086